With a Yes and A Yippee

By Richard A. Gist

Published by:

FriesenPress
Suite 300 – 852 Fort Street
Victoria, BC, Canada V8W 1H8

www.friesenpress.com

Distributed to the trade by The Ingram Book Company

Cover Photo: Author and his dad, 1936

Dedicated to Norma,
The Constant Yes and
Yippee of my life.

Table of Contents

Preface

....

(or is it an Introduction?)

I wrote this book in 1997, the year I retired, and it has lain undisturbed in a file since. In it I share memories, I philosophize, pontificate and preach (please, they're not the same), I ventilate and too much ramble off onto tangents, I offer an abundance of what my detractors call blather, and here and there feebly attempt to be humorous. It clearly is not an autobiography, nor is it exactly history. I don't know what it is, but I can call it anything I like, so it's a memoir.

I've always envied people who had photos, paintings, memorabilia, and especially letters and writings from ancestors, the older the more marvelous. Nothing like that exists in my family; we have not been a particularly literate clan. As someone who knows nothing about my great-grandparents or their parents, I determined to leave something that I hope will linger among those who come after my grandchildren. Chances of that are slight, but that is my fantasy. I want one or two of my descendants to come across, no, to inherit and cherish, my meanderings as a gift from the past, as a window through which to see, however dimly, this time in their family's history, and me, by the way I describe it. Perhaps this is my attempt at claiming a bit of immortality, though I reluctantly suggest that.

I also wrote for a wider audience than those not yet born. I wrote for family and friends, though for fifteen years I elected not to share it with them. I am offering it now a bit timidly. And always, when I dribble words on paper, I write for a phantom community of imagined readers. They don't even have to be appreciative, they just have to read–a pleasant illusion. And last of all, I write for my biggest fan and critic: me. I write because I simply enjoy the process, whether it's ever read or not.

Everything in the book reflects the 1997 me. I say that because that's not who I am today. I have grown almost as much in the last fifteen years as I did in my first seventeen, which are addressed in the book. Retirement set me free to again seek and explore widely, unrestricted by the confines of the ministry, and if this memoir were written today, it would be considerably different. Nonetheless, with the smallest exceptions, I have left it as I found it. To alter it would feel like a violation of who I was.

I use the word, "book," which feels strange to me. I use it only because I wrote at length–perhaps a problem in today's world. People's reading habits have changed dramatically; they like short chapters they can whip through in a few minutes' sitting. Many communicate in 140 character tweets. I, on the other hand, live in a cave. I don't tweet, am unfamiliar with Facebook and its relatives, and have neither cable nor dish for television. I don't carry a cell phone. I enjoy the freedom of living in a world of my own making, comfortably beyond the reach of others most all the time. My writing style reflects both my personality and my past; I can run on for multiple pages, though I have included a few, one-page, "half-chapters" in the book. I can't even say it's good stuff worth the reader's time, only that I enjoyed committing my thoughts to paper. Additionally, this is not a commercial venture, so my writing has not been professionally edited, and is certainly more wordy than it might be (You're experiencing some of that already). Still, I offer it just as it is.

I have shared two of the chapters with family and friends over the years, but only recently have I again read the book as a unified whole. It has amused, even enchanted, me a bit, with its childhood fantasies, adolescent idealism, and the roots of incompatible life principles and contradictory values that it reflects. We humans have this great capacity to simultaneously maintain mismatched visions of life, and unless we work at getting to know ourselves, can maintain them for a lifetime. I've worked hard at creating a sense of wholeness in my life so was a bit intrigued at seeing how some of the inconsistencies I've confronted got their start. Does this sound strange to you, that I'm reacting to something I wrote as though it's all new to me? Yeah, I find that surprising too, though it has been my genuine experience.

In reviewing the manuscript I discovered that at least three chapters are missing; I remember writing them. Maybe there is another version of this book floating about. Also, a couple chapters might better be deleted, but I haven't done that, though they be vacuous, and thus, boring. I did make three changes in the manuscript. I eliminated the name of one person, though I tell his story, and I changed the names of two other neighbors, each, I think, for defensible reasons.

Further, I am taken by how much richness I left out, both stories and people. If members of my family look for themselves in my memories, they will largely be disappointed, as will some of my closest friends with whom I spent many an experience. I won't explain or defend that beyond saying the book just happened. I simply sat down at the keyboard and wrote what came to me, which is the process in most all my writing (I never will be charged with being organized).

For instance, if I had thought of it, I might have included this small story, which just now came to mind. I was perhaps four-and-a-half years old and was taken to Sunday school for the first time. My Sister Doris led me down the church steps to a classroom in the basement kitchen. Seven or eight rambunctious children filled all the seats at a small table; there was no chair for me. I felt out of place, left the room, left the church, and walked home.

The point of the story is not to play with my psychological reaction to the situation–there was no room for me–but rather the journey I took. At that early age I walked unescorted from one end of my hometown to the other, a distance of over a mile. I crossed a highway, walked through downtown and across Main Street, and traversed sixteen city blocks, and no one stopped me to ask where I was going or where I was coming from. As far as I can determine, no one at the church was particularly alarmed at my absence, and my older siblings simply assumed I had returned home.

We have had seven decades to grow and improve as a society, and yet such an undisturbed excursion by a four-year-old today would be unlikely. Not only was I safe, everyone assumed I would be. My great-grandchildren are largely denied that sense of security, and today many parents live on the edge of caution, if not fear, for their little ones. Without question, a missing four-year-old would be cause for panic. But I was part of a blessed generation that lived in a less complicated time under trustworthy conditions that formed us, and in part, explain who we are today. I hope something of that presents itself in what follows.

The North End

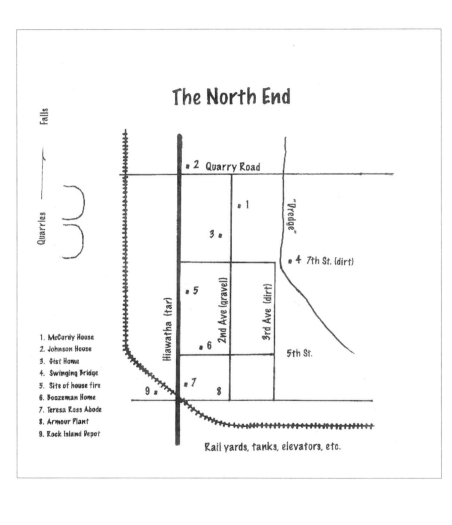

Falls

Quarries

"Dredge"

2 Quarry Road

1

3

4 7th St. (dirt)

Hiawatha (tar)

2nd Ave (gravel)

3rd Ave (dirt)

5

6

5th St.

9

7

8

1. McCurdy House
2. Johnson House
3. Gist Home
4. Swinging Bridge
5. Site of house fire
6. Boozeman Home
7. Teresa Ross Abode
8. Armour Plant
9. Rock Island Depot

Rail yards, tanks, elevators, etc.

Chapter One

With a Yes and a Yippee!

Many years ago I created a "Convivial Conception Day" card (anyone can send the birthday variety). The large C in "convivial" lent an alluring curved line to the top edge of the card. On the inside this same seductive arc became part of an enthroned egg before whom, from all appearances, knelt her royal subjects. On second glance one realized (I hoped) that the forms were not motionless, but rather represented the feverish, squiggling rush of sperm to cross the page, each intent on reaching the throne first. I have no recollection of what scandalous doggerel I penned, if any, but it did occur to me that the momentous occasion of conception rarely rated a mention, much less a card or a cake. For that one time, at least, I remedied the oversight.

One should be aware of one's conception day. God filled it with Mystery. Of course, we never can be sure of the date, unless mom put Xs on the calendar, and the Xs were spaced out sufficiently to eliminate other life-offering possibilities. In such cases her information might be trustworthy, although my mother never would have owned up to such record keeping, or even the event itself that could be registered. That was the circumspect way of her generation. So, we conception-day-seekers must content ourselves to following the mathematical trail back and cautiously claiming a date. If I entered this world in orderly fashion then my conception day was Saturday, February 24, 1934. Because my dad worked sixty and seventy hour weeks, it seems a likely time. Saturday night. Bath Night. Uninsulated house. From midnight to midnight the temperature outside was bone chilling, a good time to retire early. Or stay awake later.

I don't know what my dad's workweek was like prior to my conception except that he most certainly skinned a few, grease-smeared knuckles in exchange for his wages. His day as an auto mechanic at Totman's Auto began at 7:00 a.m. It ended when the work was done, often nine, ten, even eleven o'clock at night.

My mother's lonely challenge included keeping a drafty house clean, preparing meals from scant ingredients, and mothering her brood of a son and three daughters, perhaps thankful she did not have yet a fifth little one to nurture. On that cold evening after getting her children bedded down, she probably was thankful to have a chance to relax and cuddle, though I doubt she consciously intended an invitation to me.

On a larger scale, my conception day concluded the end of the first week of the United States Army delivering the airmail. The commercial contract for the fledgling airmail system was momentarily tied up in a political knot, and the army had stepped in to keep the mail moving. Five airmen lost their lives in the process and some in Congress were crying "legalized murder" in the highly partisan debate over the issue. With typical military-mindedness the Army Air Chief said that five deaths were not excessive. Not for him, at least. His seeming indifference to another's death and the tentative promise of my birth, occurred that day.

The world obviously did not miss a beat just because I got my start. My beloved Gophers lost a basketball game to Iowa that day, 33-30, and in my home town people plopped down two-bits at the Orpheum to see Cecil B. Demille's, *Four Frightened People*, starring Claudette Cobert and Herbert Marshall. At what precise point in that movie did the promise of me happen? Or was it during the cartoon, or some "short subject?" I enjoy pondering such imponderables.

How fortunate we were with people freely enjoying the movies and babies being conceived, for in far-off Europe that day something surreal unfurled. All across Germany, through the wonder of radio, over one million Germans took a step already assumed by three million other of their fellow citizens. Led by Rudolph Hess, simultaneously, one of out every 60 Germans took the following oath: "I swear unshaken fidelity to Adolph Hitler and unquestioning obedience to him and the leaders designated for me by him." Madness conceived over the airwaves, but also hope in unnumbered wombs, including one in the "McCurdy House" on Second Avenue North in Pipestone, Minnesota.

I like the advantage conceptions have over births. They are private affairs, and little distinguishes one from the other; not color or ethnicity, or even species. Although abounding in number, for a time they remain God's precious secret. All of them. They are *mirabile dictu* experiences, but only heaven celebrates them. (By the way, if you do not know the wonderful to relate phrase in the above sentence, take time to look it up. Not only does it carry delightful baggage, but it rolls off the tongue like few other words that we can put together.)

Conception is also one of Earth's greatest extravagances. Involved are a solitary, virginal egg, and maybe a hundred or so million anxious little sperm (one-hundred-twenty million is perhaps average). How should one categorize sperm? They're obviously alive, but are they something less than life? Do we classify human sperm as human life even though they are only half the equation? Can we speak of half-life in any meaningful way? Hundreds of millions of these tiny, long-tailed fellows perish each time they are catapulted into action. Yet, no one ever carries placards on their behalf.

What a carnival with so many of them frantically rushing toward the same goal, a prize only one, possibly two, may claim. What an achievement, to be the first among uncounted legions. I wonder a bit about the one in last place. Nothing should have to finish one-hundred-millionth in any kind of race. I suspect that little guy worked as hard as the one who won, and yet all he got for his efforts was a face full of flagellating tails. Of course in this race you either take first place or you lose. One winner, 119,999,999 losers, all flushed into oblivion. Why so many? Could not one determined guy do it alone? Or maybe a hundred push each other to cross the finish line first? As I understand it, each sperm carries similar messages all coded up in genetic language. So why all this superfluity of participants? Is the journey so difficult and perilous that only sheer numbers insures occasional success? Is there a doctor in the house? Fortunately it takes place clandestinely. It really is quite sobering to contemplate.

By contrast, births are more public and subject to the whims and disease of this world. Life can betray a birth. Although multitudes are born to peaceful, loving, homes, elsewhere malnutrition, disease, and war cradle newborns. And the stillborn breathe not a breath of this world's sweet air.

One of this world's tragic, but certainly not unmatched, stories came out of the Nuremberg Trials following World War II. As part of Hitler's Final Solution for those who dared be born Jewish, prisoners were routinely marched to the gas chambers. At Wilna, Poland, a very few escaped, and some lived in graves in a nearby Jewish cemetery. Under the cloak of darkness these people would emerge to become one of the world's most tragic communities. One night a young woman from this aberrant group gave birth to a baby boy. The eighty-year-old gravedigger, "wrapped in a linen shroud," helped deliver the baby. Shortly a cluster of ragged, half-starved Jews gathered around. The sight of that new life reawakened within the old man a long dormant hope. In hushed and reverent tones he ventured that this must be the Messiah, for who but He could be born in the lap of Death? The mother, however, unable to provide milk for her little one could only respond to his weakening cries by feeding him her tears.[1]

One of the steps leading to this lawless outrage was taken on my conception day as members of my species pledged unquestioning allegiance to a narcissistic megalomaniac (people almost never recognize them) who pursued the monstrous concept of redemptive violence. Whoever said it first got it right—"Owe unqualified allegiance to no man."

In such a world where life is so consistently degraded, conception seems refreshingly clean. Each life-forming instant enjoys God's marvelous let-there-be-ness. The Divine Mystery says, "Let there be . . . uh, squirrelness," and strands of DNA embrace one another, genes excitedly and randomly pairing up. "Let there be hippopotamus-ness" (I just had to give you the challenge of saying that) and again it all happens. I speak of "-ness" to distinguish life from *a* life, the spiritual energy of being from the process of becoming a uniqueness of personality and soul.

Two Gospel accounts assert that Jesus was conceived by the Holy Spirit. But all life is. Life is the marvel of Divine energy and the substance-of-earth coming delightfully together. And such miracles need musical accompaniment. What, I wonder, is the sound of conception? It must be the sound of heaven sympathetically vibrating in the earth-bound egg. God dances a nifty step among the clouds, points a power-laden finger, first here, then there, and half-shouting, half-singing, cries, "Let there be!" Each time the Earth trembles in ecstasy and responds with a "Yes!" and a "Yippee!" Conception resonates with the harmonies of joy, affirmation, and promise. It happens with pigs and elephants and polar bears. It happens with humans. Each and all are given the untamed possibility to become, and to become aware. Wow! No greater gift exists in the entire Universe. The heavens must be filled with both orchestra and choir.

I hesitate to speak of souls in all this. Too many people have too much to say about such mysteries. They argue interminably without ever getting around to clarifying terms (and few embrace the Biblical understanding of soul as "life" or "living being," human or otherwise). Some raise their voices and blood pressure to dangerous heights, so it must be important to them, but over what do they fight? Mostly they speak of souls in the third-person-neuter, as an "it," something God passes out to human babies, now days, human fetuses, to elevate them above all other furred and four-legged creatures. Riddle: "What is small enough to fit inside a single human cell, yet too big to squeeze into an elephant's skin?" Yes, of course, a soul.

Most people don't realize that we create our worlds–which are largely illusion–with words. I cannot find on this planet a single thing I can apply the word "s-o-u-l" to. I've looked everywhere. But if I use the word, I then

1. Paul Tillich, The Shaking of the Foundations, Pelican Books, 1962, pp. 166f.

create in my world what isn't there. I do it all the time. So do you. For instance, people do what they do, but if I call their actions, "sin," I create sin in my world. But it's an illusion, a product of the mind. I use the word "evil," but my dog doesn't experience evil, because it's not real, and he's gifted only to see what is real. God too. God doesn't buy into our illusions. (Shakespeare had Hamlet put our self-deceptions into words: "There is nothing good or bad but that thinking makes it so.") In over thirty years of pre-marital counseling, in a simple exercise I put every couple through, only once, I'll say it again, *only once in over thirty years,* did I find a person who could actually see what was real. Everyone else offered illusion in place of sight. Virtually no one saw their partners, only their illusions about their partners. No wonder so many marriages struggle when people marry their fantasies.

Still, I know the language of "soul." I can use the word like everyone else. The concept of soul is a little tougher, however. When the fertilized egg begins sub-dividing, it takes the route of all creation, articulating the "one" in a variety of remarkable ways. The first cell is precisely duplicated billions of times, and yet the mystery of individualization takes over as identical cells miraculously express themselves as blood and tissue and bone and hair and brain. Inexplicably couched within this mystery (or along side of it) is the wonder of a mind, the promise of a personality, the impatient secret of spirit. We don't have minds or bodies or spirits, we are those things, and when the three exist in harmony we experience wholeness, that is, health. The pasting of a soul upon or into this unity appears to me as religious excess, arising from the kind of theology that too often appears on bumper stickers. Lifting up human beings by giving them a soul perpetuates the arrogant and sometimes desperate attempt so evident in the Christian Tradition where the *imago Dei* (the image of God) was overemphasized in order to elevate ourselves above the beasts, and consequently, in the eyes of God. But even an earthworm is in the image of the Creator, and Earth would suffer far more if tomorrow all the earthworms were to disappear, than it would if the human family were to do so.

If I *have* a soul, I have no idea where I keep it or what it looks like. I don't know where my wife Norma keeps hers either. And poor Sammy, our dachshund, has none. His gift of life is without spiritual pockets; there is no place to secret a soul. They are dispensed only to humans, don't you see, which leaves me with the dilemma of explaining why I experience so much soulness in Sammy.

In my childhood life was simpler. A baby was a precious life that you cuddled, and which reacted to facial expressions, and cooed and cried and dirtied its flannel diapers. Before entering this world it was not yet a baby, at least in our thinking. Similarly, my family's eggs came from a back yard, chicken pen where the rooster energetically busied himself with rooster callings. I remember many occasions where I thought he was beating up on a hen, and sometimes, in sympathy to the hen, I would interrupt the proceedings. In spite of my misguided efforts, however, most of the eggs we ate probably were fertilized, but no one would have suggested we were eating chicken; they were eggs. And one would have been declared a bit crazy if he or she entered a cafe and asked for two chicks "sunny side up." If I sound cynical in my clumsy attempt to be facetious, it's only because I believe all life is of God and equidistant from the heart of the Creator. Elevating our species over others by giving us souls is a discount of the miracle of God in all life. The reason God knows when a sparrow falls to the ground is because God is one with the sparrow, as with all life.

If we must debate souls, and I know the jeopardy of entering the fray, I would argue that the gift of life is a *given*; the soul, a delightful *happening*. That which took shape at my conception was not me. I hadn't happened yet. The I that is me is not a satisfied egg, or blood and tissue, or even pulsing electrical current. Nor enzymes. Nor even the spiritual fabric of an attached soul. I am the creation of time. I have been formed, not in the womb, but in the kitchen and bathroom and at the dining-room table. In school, in worship, on the playground and in the theater. I am an accumulation of experiences from which I draw conclusions. I am an unfolding and growing history with emotions and relationships. I am a bit of my mother and dad, brother and sister, neighbor and neighborhood bully. I am my memories and dreams, my frustrations and accomplishments. I am the mystery referred to as Dick or Richard, even the Reverend Mr. Gist, for goodness' sake. If God preserves anything of me it must be these things. If God preserves less or other than these it will not be me. Unless . . . unless, I was preexistent, already a heavenly being, and I chose to be born into this world, into my family and circumstances. Otherwise the idea of a soul without a history makes no sense to me. And my Christian Faith and those making bold declarations about souls, typically do not embrace preexistence, though we all might give reincarnation a closer look; it provides answers to questions our Christian Faith truly struggles with. Having said that, I firmly believe all things and occurrences are in the loving hands of the Creator; nothing is in jeopardy, nothing is lost.

On the other hand, Church history holds too many ugly reminders of religion's self-serving audacity in declaring others to be without souls, to lie outside of God's care. Women; a variety of dark-skinned, indigenous peoples beyond Europe; and of course, all animals, have taken their turns at being disdainfully discounted as vacuous, though often useful, life forms, doomed to exist without lasting meaning. The human family's soul-filled superiority has provided license for ceaseless violence and theft.

Imprisonment, enslavement, and slaughter have been the byproducts of soul-possession, an imagined superiority that effectively blinds the "spiritually blessed" to the mystery, beauty, and pricelessness of all life, including their own. That is why in conception I speak of God declaring "squirrelness" and "humanness." Conception, for all its spiritual beauty, is but a promise, and not one always kept. If I were given a soul, like an ornament placed on a Christmas tree, the world pays too high a price for the privilege extended to me. On the other hand, if I grow into soulfulness, embracing fully the gift of Creation and self, honoring life in all it exotic forms, and daily giving thanks for the whole of it, maybe I can become something called a soul. But it is just words we are playing with. I am a part of life, not a lord over it. But what a stunning existence. *Gloria in excelsis deo!*

I lost a beautiful dog some years ago. He died an excruciating death in a ghastly, double-springed conibear trap. Some people actually design and make such devices and others use them (and the Law defends them), and still others buy and wear the skins that are "harvested" through their use. The one that killed "Li'l Hen" was so powerful, it had to be set with a vice. In his case, he, like all animals who respond to the bait in such land-set traps, was seized, then slowly squeezed to death in its ever-tightening jaws. I could do nothing to prevent it. Furiously wrestling with the monstrous thing in the dark I lacked both the knowledge and the physical strength to open it. The responding police officer could not open it either. I buried and grieved Henry. It was not lost dogginess I mourned, though the destroying of all life inflicts me with pain, it was him, a canine personality, a long, sleek, black, four-legged soul if you will.

As a cleric I remain uncomfortable with the religious jargon circulating around this issue (and am surprised my writing process led me here; it was not my intention). One of my sisters experienced the unleashed pain of a stillbirth, another one no less than seven spontaneous abortions. In each case, dreams and emotional investment and an imagined new life were ripped away. Something priceless was denied its promise, innocent life its opportunity. That mysterious, sacred gift of life had been denied the opportunity to become a person, a living soul. Some people cannot conceive of a human life without a soul. For me, the difficult part remains a soul void of a person. I do not know how to handle blank, unimprinted spirit. We are not given a soul, we are given the opportunity to become such. In the end, do any of us know of what we speak and argue?

I stand ignorant before the Mystery, but in my cluelessness declare that there is but one Giver and one Gift, taking unending forms, and somehow all is One. Just as every cell in the body sings the tune of the first cell, so all life, in its wondrously varied forms, vibrates with the energy of God. Life is the gift to be celebrated, not soul, that so consistently, often unknowingly, collaborates with Pain, Terror, and Death.

We are now harvesting body parts from pigs. To my knowledge no one is suggesting that such options should not be options. This gets deep very quickly for one such as I. Given the situation, let's say, a wife with a failing heart, I might very well call for a heart valve from a pig, and be deeply thankful for it. The ethical question, however, is should I even be given that option? Should I, as a human being, be able to assume that the miracle of my conception and the essence of my being somehow out-shines that of other beings; that my yes and yippee were shouted more clearly because with human language? Do I want my departure forestalled through killing? In every way possible I resist becoming partners with Death. Supposedly, in comparison with a pig, I'm the responsible party, yet can I rightfully make it responsible for me? At the cost its life? Life's partner is Death, and this world's swine are not responsible for that. God is. Or, for the non-religious, circumstances are. As an articulate human being I have the power to put into words, "A human is special. A human has a soul. A human has the unlimited right to create saviors from pigs." For many, to be able to say it makes it so. I choose not to be part of that. It's the kind of soul-filled yet soulless reasoning that leaves young mothers with nothing but tears for their babies. In this world we have too many self-proclaimed superior beings, and far too much killing. It's amazing how much the religious concept of soul gets entangled in all of this.

So, I use the words and speak about people having souls, but I never fool myself into thinking someone else knows what I mean by such, for I surely do not. One thing I do know, however; life is the kind of gift, the kind of mystery that cannot be owned. To make the attempt borders on the monstrous. Being can only be related to. Freely killing those we have power over, as though we rightfully possess their being, is porno-graphic and a contradiction of the Oneness out of which we all flow, the Wholeness that cradles us each one. With or without the imposition of soul, every conception has the fingerprints of God upon it.

I'm one of the lucky ones. My conception resulted in a life, my life. That should be enough miracle for one person, even if it is cut short. Just to be, and to be aware, in an unending Universe. Wow! Wow! Wow! To think of it causes me to hold my breath. Still, I've selfishly known moments when I wished that God on that cold night in 1934 had treated me differently. My genes might have been paired up in more attractive or powerful ways. But no, what I am, for this I was conceived. In response to God's cry of "Let there be," something within my mother responded, "Yes!" . . . and . . . . "Yippee!" If my life is to be anything more than an event "writ in water," my task, then, is to keep the response echoing in the rooms of my being and through the corridors of this uncertain world.

And here's the kicker. I was born into this world's most violent and destructive species. What is the spiritual significance of that? How do I deal with that? In ways both subtle and probing, that slowly became an overriding interest of my later years, and may find slight expression in these chapters. Or not. I suddenly realize I have carried on a bit much here. I will guard against that as I continue.

Chapter One and One Half

....

Christmas, 1934

Christmas Day, less than six weeks following my birth, my mother visited her sister's family. They, too, lived in Pipestone. We Gists were poor, our relatives nearly destitute. While there, my mother watched my cousin, who was almost four, play with her Christmas present–a five cent wash rag. She carefully smoothed it out on her lap, then folded and patted it, folded and patted it a second time, shook it out, rubbed it on her cheek, held it up to admire, proudly showed it to my mom, turned it over and examined the other side, and then began folding it again. Her very own wash rag. Are not children unbelievably beautiful. Small wonder Jesus told us to be like them.

Chapter Two

....

"Just Arrived"

Children, and probably all creatures, are born with the marvelous capacity to accept their surroundings. Knowing nothing else, they innocently approve of their life circumstances as the way life is. Their eyes filter everything through wonder, and if security and love are a part of their world, then the world itself, no matter its content or where it is found, becomes wonder-full. *Place*, known intimately, becomes one of our earliest spiritual resources. As we age we too often ignore the importance of spirit-filled spaces, but in childhood it is essential to have them. Children born to unrelenting abuse, overwhelming poverty, or the horrors of war are robbed of the spiritual foundation that "place" gives. Never knowing that first, wonderful, sheltering corner of the Creation makes it more difficult to find all the other wonderful corners in later years. But if we inherit the spirituality of place, no matter what its makeup, we truly can never be thrown out of this world.

My early place was poorly accommodated, and innocently accepted. Although our family was poor, at least by worldly standards, I never knew it. My older siblings remember the hard times of the Great Depression; they knew the drudgery that accompanied our parents' fears and concerns—How do we pay the bills? How do we feed the children?—but also gratefully acknowledge that our home was secured with love. Somehow mom and dad managed to spiritually bless our beginnings, though they never would have described it that way.

Poverty must be fought against or it triumphs. One of my mother's programs of survival was the universal one; she raised a garden. Not only to set food on the table, but to earn income. She planted and maintained a huge tomato patch, almost daily hoeing, watering, and doing battle with infestations, right down to the harvest. People in town said she had the best tomatoes around, due, perhaps, to the rich soil of the ten-year flood plain on which we lived, but attributable also to the hundreds of gallons of water she pumped and carried to the plants during the hot, summer months. In late summer she gave the family income a nudge up by selling tomatoes for fifty-cents a bushel.

Mom was a Brown, the daughter of Abijah and Elma. Her dad was a harness maker. The blood of Scotland, Ireland, Holland, France and Germany (that we knew of) pulsed through her veins. At the time we had no idea "what" dad was, so we never entered those prideful discussions regarding nationality that so defined and furrowed the cultural landscape of Minnesota. Germans, and especially Scandinavians, were always touting their heritages. We Gists had nothing of which to boast.

Although she had been a carrot-top in childhood, mom's hair was dark brown by the time I knew her. She stood about 5' 2". When I look at old photographs of her I'm surprised that she wasn't fat, because I always saw her that way. So much for childhood perspective. Like dad, she never had the advantage of formal education, attending school only through the fourth grade.

Those early years must have been awesomely difficult for her because she was an accomplished worrier; the circumstances of the Depression could only have added great weight to the burdens she so effortlessly created for herself. She died too soon at 56 and I've always assumed the worry contributed to her early death. Only later did I suspect she suffered from OCD (Obsessive-compulsive Disorder), something that runs in our family.

Anyway, tomatoes and other garden vegetables, fresh and canned, were staples at the Gist table. Meat was not. The demands of the Depression had nudged it right off the menu, at least until the day mom told dad that they simply had to find some way to give the children some. They looked to their budget, siphoned off a few pennies from this item, a few more from that one, and found a way to do it. At that point a family tradition was launched. Sunday was designated as meat day. In my growing up years the Sunday meal was always the finest of the week, as it was for most families, and the menu seldom varied: roast beef, potatoes and gravy, vegetables, bread or buns (often home made), and dessert, usually pie. I loved the potatoes, which we called worms, because we ran them through a ricer. Only as I grew older and no longer asked for worms did we shift to mashed potatoes. The tradition got started in humbler fashion, however. In the early thirties when it began, it became my sister Betty's task to run to the store each Saturday to pick up the meat for Sunday dinner—one-half pound of ground sausage. Whether mom and dad partook or whether only the four children did, I don't know.

Clearly, life was uncluttered by excess, and unexpected events could quickly graduate to crises. One year my brother Kenny was struck down with polio and the house was quarantined for two weeks. Because this happened when dad was at work, and because it was essential that he be at work, the heavy nursing burden fell to mom. During the quarantine dad came and went through the bedroom window and the family talked to him, and he to them, only from separate sides of the closed door.

Fortunately Kenny overcame the illness with only slight physical damage. Then he and Shirley, the youngest of my three sisters, came down with pneumonia. Shirley had double pneumonia. A live-in nurse was hired to care for them, and after a week's time the family had run up a bill of forty-dollars, with nothing with which to pay it. Dad turned to his employer, who always was good to his employees, and borrowed the money. Mom worked off Doc Coombs bill by washing his office linen, and then went to scrubbing floors at the Royal Hotel to help meet the other mounting bills. To do the latter she had to take me with her, and one of the stories I grew up on was how I came into the hotel from the sidewalk, chomping away on something, and when mom quizzed me about it I showed her the gum I had picked up from off the sidewalk.

Our family moved to Pipestone because dad found a mechanic's job there with Totman's Auto. He had started farming in Muarry County just as the depression hit, but when corn dropped to a few cents a bushel, he went busted. For a time he commuted back and forth by train from Walnut Grove to Stillwater, where he found employment, and then closer to home, in Marshall. The family moved to Marshall in time for their fourth child, my sister Shirley, to be born. Later dad found a promising job in Pipestone, with Totman's Auto, and he began what for him became a life-long career of working on cars.

Dad was a product of a Mississippi River town in Kentucky. He attended school off and on through the third grade. Later, at the age of 16 he left home to "ride the rails" for two years before returning home to his family, which had now moved into southwestern Minnesota. Dad hung 145 pounds on a well proportioned body, was physically active, and some would say, bordering on handsome. Evidently my mother thought so, because when he asked her to go to the Muarry County fair with him, she said yes, and that was the beginning of a union that lasted until mom's death at fifty-six

In Pipestone, Totmans paid their employees on commission, and the employees worked for as long as it took to get the work done. The workday began early, and as I've already indicated, ended at nine, ten, even eleven o'clock at night. Dad was elated when he came home to proudly show his wife his first paycheck--almost nineteen dollars. That story I got from my mother. The story remembered by my brother was the week the Totmans apologetically handed him a check for $9.20, realizing it was not enough to keep a family going. My parents' anguish was considerable as they wondered how they would make all their commitments. What they did Kenny does not remember, but their worried discussions stuck in his mind. Not long after this dad's boss realized that the commission work was not always dependable (and of course he did not always get his money either), and he established a twelve-dollar-a-week minimum salary for his employees, and thus a consistency of income sufficient to keep the Gists honorable. In my growing up years I never heard dad speak of the Totman family in anything but glowing terms.

It was during this time that President Roosevelt inaugurated a commodities program, but dad would not permit someone else to pay his way. In 1938, when the personal property taxes were based on automobiles and household furnishings, our taxes were eight cents. I've pondered whether dad paid it with a dime or with a nickel and three pennies. The tax was based on 30¢ per one hundred dollars of value, so my parents total worldly possessions were valued at less than twenty-seven dollars, hardly middle class status at any time in America. Nonetheless, he and mom managed to keep the wolf from the door. Roosevelt's commodities program, however, rescued some people who had to accept help or watch their families go hungry. My two older sisters, Doris and Betty, remember being caught in the middle, between the "hads and the had-nots."

For instance, one neighbor was a postal worker and his income was steady. The kids from that family would sit in the ditch on their side of the road and tease my sisters that they had graham crackers to eat. The Gists did not. That was not very kind of the them, but then they were not always the nicest kids anyway; the oldest girl in that family took delight in filling my sister Shirley's diapers with sand at every opportunity. For my sisters, however, insult was added to injury when their cousins would come to visit, cousins who *were* receiving commodities. They would pull out large, juicy, red apples to munch on while my sisters had only the scrawny and sour, green apples from the less than robust trees in our back yard.

In those early years my brother and three sisters slept together in the kitchen on a leather couch that pulled out into a bed. Its questionable comforts were enhanced with a feather tic, one I was privileged to sleep on, sometimes under, years later. Tics are the eighth wonder of this world. Not to jump onto one and have it billow up around you with the warmth and softness that only goose down can produce is to have missed one of life's special pleasures. Bedrooms often would get down to freezing at night, but a feather tic protected all who snuggled beneath it.

It was indeed a different world, with people sleeping in kitchens. However, for two years I slept in our bathroom. When the folks bought their very own home in 1940, my brother and I shared one bed and one bedroom, my three sisters a single bed in a second bedroom. In 1943 Kenny went off to war. My sisters were older and needed more room and were allowed the luxury of expanding into "the boy's room." And I, the youngest, the spoiled one, got my very own space in the downstairs bathroom. It was a large bathroom, though not yet finished as it later would be.

My parents' small bedroom adjoined the bathroom, and because of the arrangement of bedroom furniture, the bedroom door was never closed. This allowed my sister Shirley to drive mom and dad nuts with her nightly, bedtime ritual. A typical teenager, she spent much time fussing with face and hair. Her routine included wetting her hair at the sink on the west wall, turning on the faucet for a spurt of water, then clump, clump, clumping over to the mirror on the opposite wall to set a pin curl, then clumping back to the sink, swish, then clump, clump, clump, a process repeated over and over. I enjoyed the sleep of the innocent and never heard it, but mom and dad did, did, did. By the way, I can't remember ever telling another soul that I grew up sleeping in the bathroom.

Few young people today know about feather tics, nor are they familiar with flour sack dresses, but they were common in the thirties and forties, as common as the long, brown, cotton stockings both boys and girls wore over long underwear, which were held up with garters. Now when you say flower sack, and later it also was feed sacks, don't envision a piece of cloth that has "Miller's Flour" printed on it. The material was patterned, and sometimes quite nicely so; everyone was trying to help out in those depression years, and besides, to get not only flour but dress material in a single purchase, certainly helped sales. Each of my sisters had two dresses with matching panties made from the sacks. The poor elsewhere did also. One outfit was worn while the other was in the wash, and in leapfrogging clean over dirty, little girls were kept presentable.

I've gotten ahead of myself and want to reset the clock to 1934, the height of the depression. At some point that year mom had to give expression to those heavily loaded words, "Honey, I'm pregnant." Whether mom and dad intended to have more children, I do not know; in those days you simply took what God gave. Still, the fact that through the early years of the Great Depression mom had avoided getting in a family way suggests that they were in some kind of holding pattern. I must have been an unwanted accident, though a wonderful one, to be sure.

Recently my wife Norma and I stopped at a restaurant in Milaca, Minnesota. When we entered a woman at some distance began waving at us. Realizing that she thought she knew us I turned in her direction so she could get a better look at me. She continued to wave. I ignored her attempt to get our attention, so she jumped up from the booth she shared with two other women, and bustled over to us. When it became apparent that she was going to give me a hug I raised my hands in self-defense and said, "I know you think you know me, but you are mistaken." She stood there looking at me, eyes wide, mouth agape, not believing I was not her brother. Her two companions also could not believe I was not him. I even talked like him. Very foolishly I did not get her name or the name of her brother, but some time later I checked the birth records in the Pipestone County Court House just in case I was one of two and my parents could only afford the one. Unless a twin birth was kept out of the public record (which might be possible) I came into the world solo; according to the records, as legitimate, though it's hard to conceive of any other kind of birth.

I have a friend who was placed in an orphanage at the age of three, not because he was an orphan, not because he was unloved, but because his parents could not afford to keep him. During the Depression wrenching situations led many parents to farm out their children to relatives, and occasionally to strangers, the older ones to work for their keep, the younger ones as foster children of sorts. Such was a reality of the time.

One of mom's bedtime stories described the torture of a mother struggling with just that kind of decision, that of giving away one of her children. After putting the children to bed one night, she went from bed to bed, and rehearsed the special qualities and vulnerabilities of each child, attempting to determine which one would be given up. Of course she could not decide. Each child was special and she loved each one so completely, that giving one away was out of the question. My mother told me the story more than once. Had she struggled with such a decision? Did she think I needed reassurance? I didn't. I didn't know our circumstances were desperate. Perhaps it was she who had the need to reassure me. Whatever the motivation involved, the story was a favorite, not of poverty or struggle, but simply of love. I needed no reassurance; all was well in my universe. We were poor, but the world was rich. Our environment was lean, but never degraded.

Joyfully welcomed or not, I arrived at 3:55 on a wet, autumn afternoon, and I cannot imagine being born into a more wonderful place and time, even though I happened on the "North End," literally on "the other side of the tracks." My hometown had tentatively pushed its way north over the rail yards of the Rock Island and the Milwaukee and Omaha Railroad lines, but quickly pulled back, evidently deciding it was a bad idea. The north end of town was like an experiment that fizzled. First two blocks wide, then dwindling to one, it was an area defined by three avenues, Hiawatha, Second, and Third, or in our terminology, "the tar road," "the gravel road," and "the dirt road." Hiawatha was the only street connecting the North End to "town," and was probably paved because it drove all the way to the Government Indian School a mile north of town. Our neighborhood was conveniently along the way. Had some great hand threaded a string through the south end of Hiawatha and then suspended the city from it in space, the north end would have dangled like a tail from the city. A tail, and maybe an embarrassment.

The North End (I still say the words with affection) effectively began at fourth street and the parallel Rock Island Railroad tracks, had a fifth street, but no sixth, a seventh street (dirt), but no eighth, and abruptly ended at the road that ran from Highway 75 on the east, through farm land, over the creek, and finally to the quarries which lay west of Hiawatha. I suppose this was also Ninth Avenue though we knew it as the "quarry road." Beyond Ninth lay the sometimes-cultivated fields, sometimes-pasture-land, of the Government Indian School.

Fifth street, stretching between Hiawatha and Second Avenue, provided the sparse evidence that the town had at one time tried. The north side of Fifth had a neat row of five, carefully placed houses that were actually fronted with a sidewalk (no curbs existed north of the tracks). Indeed, the Boozeman house was proudly of brick with two cement lions guarding the front steps. Sixty years later they still faithfully repose there. When I was little the very pleasant couple who lived in this luxurious home also had a birdhouse out front that was designed to look like the real house. It greatly impressed me. Inside on the mantel was a ship in a bottle, an even more remarkable wonder. The Boozemans were the richest people I knew, and kind to we ragamuffins in the neighborhood.

Indeed, Fifth Street had the appearance of having been planned, a real anomaly for the North End, for the rest of our neighborhood fell into place haphazardly. In my time there were more empty lots than houses. Two tarpaper shacks squatted down by the creek. Another family lived in a railroad boxcar. Seventh Street, which was dirt, abided a house with a dirt floor, an area typically under water in the Spring. We had the obligatory, vacant, unpainted, two-storied house with the broken windows, the Armour chicken processing plant, a greenhouse that occupied a full city block, a junk yard, and the creek. It was a neighborhood where most everyone kept large gardens, and many, as did we, kept chickens in the back yard. Two families raised pigs. Growing up, it was close to Paradise.

On the far north end of Second Avenue sat the McCurdy house. There in the east bedroom I most probably was conceived, and most certainly was born. The house consisted of a large kitchen, small living room, and two tiny bedrooms. It boasted an open front porch and a washroom on the back. It was through the window of that east bedroom that dad crawled in and out during the quarantine. That was two years before my birth. It also was out that window that I fell as a toddler, down through the open cellar door to the concrete steps below. I had never heard that story until I confirmed with my brother the date of his illness. He told me how frightened my mother had been as I was covered with blood, but seemingly none the worse for the happening. It's marvelous how durable little people are; also marvelous the things that surface when one asks an older brother questions.

Our family rented this house for fifteen dollars a month from the McCurdy family. The place was storybook, as fresh and wonderful as depression poor could be. The house sat alone on a city block of lawn, trees, garden, and overgrowth. Great elms shaded the house and most of the front yard, and a large clump of lilacs stood along what would have been Eighth Street had there been one, lilac bushes that never bloomed. To the east was the struggling apple orchard of three trees, and north of that the vigorous garden. All the way to the north end sat a small barn with an open lean-to where dad parked our *Whippet*. In between the house and the barn, paralleling second avenue, a line of black walnut trees stood at attention.

I learned to use a hammer bashing open stubborn walnut shells. We had an 8 X 8 inch block of wood about ten inches long that we stood on end for this. It had been used for so long that it had a little hollow place worn into it that cradled the walnut so it would not squirt away when you hit it. That was essential since I needed both hands to swing the hammer. Sadly, few people plant black walnut trees any more; they measure time much to casually for an impatient world. But they are a marvelously faithful tree, and generous with their exotic fruit.

The house itself was as common as dust, pure Americana, complete with the aforementioned cellar door, and a well pump on the concrete slab that we called the back porch. For the older children pumping water was a daily chore, for me a constant tease. I would swing from the handle world without end, but never could I coax a drop of water from the ground. I never tired of trying though. And in one expeditious lesson I joined that great cloud of witnesses who testify to the enduring truth that one never puts tongue to cold pump handle in winter.

Our cellar door was friendlier than the back porch. It slanted away from the east side of the house where our hollyhocks sprawled, and offered a grand morning place in the sun. We often congregated on its weather-beaten surface to eat green apples or to dip stalks of rhubarb into saucers of sugar. My sisters would make little dancing girls from the hollyhock blossoms and buds, and line them up on the metal drip strip that ran along the top of the cellar doors. I remember kittens there, wrestling among us in foot-pumping embrace, and also old *Sport*, our dog, sprawling on the door's sun-warmed surface.

Sport was the fat of those lean years, my father's pride and the children's joy, a remarkable white and brown-spotted English Pointer. He appears in rare photographs of those early days, his tail always a blurred fan.

Sport was good at his trade of seeking out game, but also at chaperoning and protecting my brother and sisters. He took them to school in the morning and returned to meet them in the afternoon. Mr. Denniger, the Rock Island stationmaster, swore he could set his watch by the dog's afternoon trip. When the children were small and played in the vast corn-fields on the Indian School acres, dad had only to mount the outside stairs that led to the kitchen, then shout Sport's name, and the dog would leap high, head rising above the corn stalks, and yelp, locating the children and signifying that all was well. Dogs are one of God's greatest gifts to the human family.

My brother and sisters were clustered five and more years above me in the family tree, and by the time I was old enough to traipse cornfields, Sport was too old to jump. I remember him as feeble, and almost blind. Still, he was of a mind to protect the children, and in that role entered a fight with Newcomer's Chinese Chow dog one summer afternoon, only to have one eye gouged; it turned milky white. Ever after I disliked the Chow, thinking him a mean-spirited animal for being so cruel.

In this world certain people need only themselves to be unhappy. Are they born that way, or do they grow into it? I don't know. Most children have those few precious years when happiness has a chance to get rooted, in part because it is free, both of nostalgia and worries about tomorrow. Each day sits on the edge of creation, waiting to happen, and children participate in this unfolding mystery, contributing their bit to it, and absorbing the rest without editing or judgment. This quality runs very deep in the human family; even the condemned children of Hitler's concentration camps left drawings of flowers and butterflies on the barracks' walls. Far from that insanity in Germany we richly blessed children of the McCurdy House had everything we needed to be happy. We were loved. Each had been given two hands, two feet, five senses, a brain, a world to use, and the time to slowly digest it's abundant offerings. And significantly, our entire family sat down at a common table two, often three, meals a day.

A stone's throw beyond the east line of our yard ran our beloved "Dredge." The Dredge was Pipestone Creek, though we were unaware of that name. Sometime in the past the stream's meandering ways had been severely reprimanded into a straight line, probably for flood control. The process had deposited a continuous mound of dirt on each side of the stream and in the intervening years weeds and willows had grown up in such profusion that these "hills" now masqueraded as unviolated nature, wild and inviting to the neighborhood children. We called it the "Dredgeditch" (one word), the meaning of the words, "dredged ditch" never occurring to us; the "Dredge" was the creek's name and we believed its ways to be natural.

The intersection of third avenue and seventh street dead-ended at the Dredge, and there a cable, suspension, foot bridge spanned the creek. It would bounce and sway and jiggle as one walked across its sun-bleached boards, and it afforded my biggest challenge and most delightful fears as I would carefully inch across it, clinging tightly to the cable hand hold. For the older children, of course, it was a proving ground of courage as they would get it bouncing and swaying, and then gallop its length with "no hands." Sadly, some gathering of city officials deemed it important to remove the bridge before I was old enough to prove myself on it.

During warm summer afternoons we would go to the Dredge to fish for what we called crabs. For this we used pork rind (sometimes innocent grasshoppers) secured by a safety pin on the end of a string. Crayfish would latch onto the fat, and unwilling to give up such a prize, allow themselves to be slowly pulled to shore. We would catch six or eight of the silly things, fuss a bit with them, then release them for another time.

The Dredge, like the quarries that lay to the west, was a playground year around. In winter we skated on its surface, cut holes in the ice and drank of its waters, built warming fires on its sand bars, and slid down its banks on sleds. In summer we built rafts to navigate its familiar waters, and in those stretches that were indeed virgin, where giant cottonwoods grew at the water's edge, we would suspend ropes from their branches and swing over the water from bank to bank, bellowing like crazed ape-men. And with those first warm slices of spring, with the sun slanting down on the snow-free southern exposures of certain hills, we would lay in the dirty, brown grass and enjoy those vague yearnings that spring visits upon all creatures of winter.

Shortly before my birth the Gists began to get religion, sort of. Something nudged mom in that direction, and when the traveling evangelist, Jerome Fischer, came to town, she attended a couple services, and then invited the good preacher to the house for a meal. While there he baptized my brother and three sisters, in the kitchen. The Gists weren't

Church people yet, however, but how could they doubt God? The stamp of the Divine was everywhere. The wonderful benefit afforded by our innocent, largely pagan, ways was that I was born in purity. My parents' simple approach to life was that it was worthwhile to be a human being, and this was a good world in which to be one. Only later, with religious training, would I be born again into the glum world of Original Sin.

I was a Sunday afternoon baby and to my knowledge only my mother witnessed Doc McKeown spanking me into life. The thermometer climbed to 55 degrees that day, warm for November 18th, and one-half inch of rain fell. To the east, however, Walnut Grove experienced a downpour. That is part of the story because dad loaded his four children into the family Whippet, and they sloshed and slogged their way to a farm east of Walnut Grove, going through ruts deep enough that even the high-slung Whippet bottomed out at times. There they picked up Pearl Keith who would keep house for us the next two weeks. In my siblings' absence, the good doctor came and delivered me. I came in at an estimated ten pounds. When mother told the doctor she had made a trip to the outhouse shortly before his arrival he scolded her saying I could have been delivered into the bowels of that humble shack. I can't think of a more dramatic entrance, but then it could also have been a quick exit--I don't think I was a breach baby.

Even though I was born with an extra vertebrae in my back, the local populace ignored my emergence. I suspect not a soul who saw Wheeler and Woolsey in *Kentucky Kernals* at the Orpheum Theatre that night uttered a word about me. I find comfort in that. Little disturbs ongoing life. The world did its thing before I arrived, and will keep right on doing it after I leave. Unless you're the village doctor (Doc. Mckeown was killed in an automobile accident months after my arrival) life barely skips a beat at your passing, and even less so at your coming. What significance one develops derives from the space between those two, nonarresting events.

I say the world took no notice, and yet that is not quite true. Almost from the beginning, the Church, which has been so significantly a part of my life, was there. The good women of Zion Evangelical Church came to the house and threw a diaper shower me; I was literally swaddled in the cloth of the Church. All four of my siblings remember this day as the one when mom let the valuable Wearever coffee pot boil dry, ruining it forever.

In the world I entered people still buried an occasional Civil War veteran, classy women sported permanent waves, the milk man delivered his products to your door, and telephone numbers of local businesses were the likes of 7, 29, and 87. For two dollars, in advance, you could get the *Pipestone County Star* delivered to your door for a whole year. The front page of the Star alerted its readers to county meetings, poultry shows, death notices, corn-hog meets and quilt-rug affairs. From today's vantage point such sounds quaint, and one might think that people operated on "by-gosh and by-golly" rather than by intent. That wasn't true, though life *did* know a more leisurely pace. Even the woes handed out by the lumbering Depression unfolded slowly. And because we humans learn far more from hardship than we do from pleasure, life was more reasoned.

Indeed, they were hard times. The local newspapers carried numerous stories of thefts of the kinds of things people needed to survive—coal, chickens, eggs, and shoes. Even an occasional pig would disappear from some, unfortunate farmer's yard. The delinquent tax list ran to three full pages in the County Star that fall (the Gist name was not on it). Still, on the day of my birth, speaking from Tupelo, Mississippi, President Franklin Delano Roosevelt declared, "All's well with the nation." Words of encouragement for a struggling society. In reality, I stepped into a pretty fine world.

Old newspapers are like gossipy friends, and I went to the *County Star* to see if my birth was properly announced. I thought I had found it when the flatteringly prominent words, "Just Arrived," popped out at me from page one, but alas, it was only an announcement that *Ben Franklin's Five and Dime* had received a shipment of *Betty Lou Fruit Cakes,* "Each with a plate, 25¢." I did make the front page, however—"The birth of a son to Mr. and Mrs. Sam Gist of this city on Sunday is reported." You can almost hear the "ho hum" behind it. It cost my folks twenty-five dollars to get me safely into this world. Quite a bargain, I figure, even though I came without a tin platter.

Chapter Three

What's in a Name?

We've all heard the joke, "It's a good thing my parents named me John."

"Why do you say that?"

"Because that's what everybody calls me."

If only it were so simple. Everyone calls me Dick, but my parents named me Richard. My brother Kenneth named me. He was nine and into this radio personality by the name of Richard Allan, and I became Richard Allan Gist. I guess I should be thankful that I was not named Hop Harrington Gist. Stranger choices have been made for new arrivals. Like the American Puritan couple who named their little one, If-Christ-Had-Not-Died-For-Thee-Thou-Hadst-Been-Damned.[2] They experienced considerable difficulty calling him for supper, however, and in time the name streamlined to "Damned." His last name was Barebone, so he limped through life known as, "Damned Barebone." People can do outrageous things to new babies, and I am thankful for the relative discretion exercised by my family. Still, they got it wrong. I never have been a Richard, though I've managed to live with the name all these years.

Most of us can look at a person and identify a name that "fits." Out of thousands of possibilities, certain names, like style of clothing, just seem to go with certain people. "Bronko Nagurski" was a Bronko Nagurski. Likewise, certain names tend to conjure up in our minds the kind of person who rightfully should bear it. The world

2. This example and others I used, are found in Irena Chambers", The Great American Baby Almanac, Viking Studio Books, New York, 1989, p. 80.

produces a certain number of natural Brutuses, so too, Marys, Cliffords, and poor souls, Hortenses.

Babies are a one-of-a-kind happening who will have unique personalities and traits that should be considered before a name is given. We don't do it that way, of course. Proud parents send out birth announcements before a handful of diapers have been changed. The Chinese got it right and would give the child a milk name to get them started in life, and then added more names as life progressed. In our culture the name is often decided upon before the birth takes place--David if it's a boy, Debra, if a girl.

Many forces give shape to a name, some purely anomalous. My parent's union, for instance, united two families horribly restricted in their vowel pools. True, this inflicted only the baby girls, but it was nonetheless an embarrassing and impossible-to-hide deficiency. Even though camouflaged with a nickname, in time the truth would come out, and the gossip would begin. "Poor souls; they only have Es and As to work with." Unhappily, I grew up trying to shield my aunts Emma (one on each side of the family), Mabel, Ethel, Ella, and Metta from all the controversy. My mother too, whose name was Eva. Eva Mae. She was named by my grandmother, Elma. On my mother's side the boys also proved vulnerable to the impairment, and selected as wives my aunts Emma, Bertha and Ellen. An aunt I never knew was named Sarah. She died in her twenties, leaving two small children. Only my Uncle Cecil, the baby of his family, heroically broke out for the benefit of the family, and married a Louella. Reportedly, family members learned to pronounce it.

Curiously, this vowel impairment did not inflict other families of that generation. For instance, my boyhood friend's mother's name was Ruby. He also had an Aunt Pearl and an Aunt Opal. Each one the gem of their parent's eye, I'm sure.

Mom and dad partially broke free from their parent's shortcomings, by adding the letters i and y. (I have both a sister Betty Jean and a sister Shirley Ardell). Y also flourished in my generation, as evidenced by the Marys, Sallys, and Beverlys I attended school with. The Y appeared not only at the end of names, but sometimes distinctively in the middle, such as in Carolyn and Phyllis, or elegantly, almost sensuously, at the beginning, as in Yvonne.

I trust most generations of females are thankful that the American Puritan influence largely died out. I mean that strange predilection for naming a daughter Purity, Abstinence, Temperance, or Charity. The guilty parents, I suspect, hoped that the name would mold the child. That would be consistent with the Biblical understanding that words had power, and could produce what they articulated. God spoke the word "shrew," for instance, and bingo, there was a shrew. Words spoken by mortals had the same power, which is why curses and blessings were taken so seriously. So names were intended to give birth to the kind of person the name indicated. If for some reason the match was not a good one, if little "God-be-with" grew up to be a real, "God-forsaken," then a name change was made to more closely match the personality. That was easier than changing the individual.

So, when David was confronted by the churlish "Nabal," Nabal's wife, Abigal, defended him, sort of, when she said to the murderous David, "Let not my lord regard this ill-natured fellow Nabal; for as his name is, so is he; Nabal is his name, and folly is with him" (Nabal meant fool). I can't imagine parents naming their precious little one, "Fool," so most likely he earned the name later in life. You have to respect the economy in that. You know what you are dealing with beforehand. Abigail's argument was that David had no right to expect anything better from someone so named.

Of course, the world is full of Nabals who go by other names, like the Father who insisted his son be named "Joe's." His last name was Deiner. Fortunately, he did not prevail over his wife's objections.

Years ago I struck up a conversation with a pregnant waitress who hoped to have a girl so she could name her Penelope Candice. She wanted to call her, "Penny Candy" (Those below the age of fifty will have to have this interpreted for them). It reminded me of my daughter and her best friend who decided to name a new puppy "Quat," so when they wanted him they could call, "Come Quat." Dogs, of course, can better weather a name than many of we humans. Penny Candy would be fairly harmless, but it's hard to imagine the motives of the parents who named their son Benedict, when their last name was Arnold. I met him briefly in prison.

When it comes to naming I prefer the consideration exercised by friends in South Dakota who really liked the name Brett Scott for their first-born, but decided against it because he probably would grow up known as, "B. S. Newman." They were unwilling to saddle their child with that.

Many people, had they had a hand in it, would go by a different name. I'm married to a Sarah, but her parents named her Norma. She was the eleventh of twelve children and figures her parents ran out of good names or didn't take it all that seriously by the time she came along. Of course, thanks to the television series *Cheers*, when she walks in for choir rehearsal everyone shouts, "Norm!" She doesn't much like that, however. "Norm," is what I get to call her. It's not for other people's use.

Even my wife and I were not above experimenting with names, trying to come up with something distinctive for our very special, first baby. We named her after her mother, only we spelled it backwards. Amron. Amron Leigh Gist. Most people assume it's a Biblical name so we usually don't have to explain ourselves.

I was christened Richard, but thankfully the world has always called me Dick. That even appears on my Social Security card. At the age of 15, when I was about to become the stock boy in the *Hiawatha Market*, and filled out the proper, government papers, when asked for my first name I never hesitated and wrote, "Dick." Except for Mrs. Nathe, my high school social studies teacher, I've never been called Richard. I do sign that on my checks and legal documents, but always with the recognition that Richard is my legal name, not my real one. Dick allows me a casualness of personality that Richard does not. Dick is like a scarred-up, substantial old desk. Comfortable to sit at, unpretentious, sturdy. Richard, the name of kings, suggests a presence and panache I've never possessed.

One of my good friends growing up was a Richard. He looked like a Richard, talked and walked like a Richard. He was a Richard. To my knowledge, only his high school Social Studies teacher, Mrs. Nathe, called him Dick. This, however, was a fairly late occurrence in his life, and he never went through years being called "Dickie," as was I. Indeed, I still have an older sister who on occasion refers to me as "Dickie Boy." She's gotten too old to hit.

Many people have no idea how their names came to them, whether from a book, a box of cereal, or a movie marquee. Still, it adds a tasty ingredient to the story of who you are and is worth an exploration. If you cannot locate the truth you have a grand opportunity to create a romantic tale with room for humor and adventure. How you were named because of the virtual stranger who found your mother stranded in a stalled car and carried her for three miles through the worst blizzard anyone can remember to get her to the hospital. Barely on time, of course. You were born in the hallway just inside the front door. Your mother never thought to ask for the stranger's name, but before she left the hospital a cuddly teddy bear arrived from out of nowhere, with the attached note, "Hope everything worked out for you and that the baby is okay." In the way of helpful strangers, of course, no name was signed, but you just fill in the blank. Maybe you are a Teddy. See how much latitude you have to be creative. It does loose a bit of punch, of course, if your name is Mary or John. Everyone knows that names like that come from favorite aunts and vagabond uncles.

The Biblical people got it wrong, of course. A name tells us less about the person named than it does about those who do the naming. Let me offer a "for instance." As a child I had red hair. When I was 3-4 years old, teen-aged neighbor girls who frequented our home delighted in teasing me about it. The more they did the more I protested, so the more they did.

I would scream and cry and say my hair was not red but purple. I didn't know my colors yet, but anything was better than red; no one else in my world was so cursed and I thought something must be wrong with me for being so. I needed someone to pick me up and tell me it was okay to have red hair. No one ever did (I'm getting to it).

Then came the handsome Reed Persinger into my life. He always spoke to me like I was important. No talking down to me, no baby talk, like so many teen-age waitresses prefer to use with me nowadays. Even at the age of four I clearly knew and appreciated the difference; I assume that most children do. So, I greatly liked this friend of dad's.

As I write this I also am transcribing a tape my sister Doris made with my dad on his 84th birthday. I didn't even know the tape existed until a month ago, but I obtained a copy and have the pleasant experience of hearing my dad's voice again–he died eight years ago. On the tape they bring up Reed Persinger, and my sister laughs and says she and our other two sisters had a terrible crush on this man, and that there was just something very wonderful about him. That surprised me. I had never known that anyone else was affected by him; he must have been something indeed.

This very evening, I kid you not, my curiosity got the better of me and I called the only Persinger listed in the Minneapolis phone book. It turned out to be Reed's brother, a man I had never heard of before. We had a delightfully animated conversation during which I learned that Reed had recently died. An elderly man. My reaction was a curious mix of feelings. The last time I saw him he was young and vitally animated, but now he had aged and died. The memory of a spirited young man and the reality of a life lived out, has no bridge for me. Nothing in between. And something is needed. I sit here before my keyboard much aware of that.

Something else about this man made him very special. He had red hair. In that he was my savior. He not only taught me, "See my finger, see my thumb, see my fist you better run," but he also taught me that I was an okay redhead.

Did this man whom I never saw beyond the age of five make a lasting impression on me? When our first, special son was born I could think of no other name that for him would suffice. He carries his first name lightly, I hope. *Reed.*

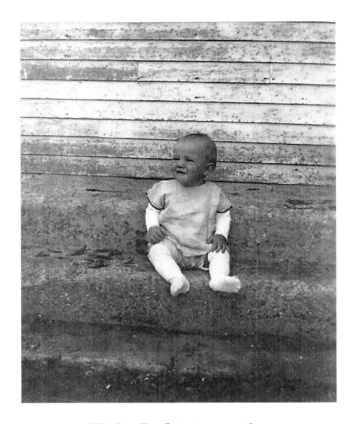

"Dickie Boy" at ten months.

Chapter Four

....

Foundations of Self

When did I happen? Where does my life start? At conception? Some would parade placards, wave Bibles, even bomb buildings, to say yes.

Or was it at my birth? That was the unquestioned premise in the world into which I was born. I was in the world. I could be touched and cradled and sung to. I was warm and soft and vulnerable, would coo and gurgle; all those things that in those days constituted a baby.

Or was it on that significant day in the house on Second Avenue? I was three. My mother was about to take me on the 125 foot walk to the outhouse. My sense is that I had resisted her earlier urgings, shaking my head that, no, I didn't have to go, though that is not part of the actual memory. But now we were on the way, me anxiously hurrying ahead of her. I was walking along the wood and leather couch with its brass tacks, the one that sat in the kitchen, the one that could be pulled out into a bed. Then it happened; my body betrayed me; I dirtied my pants. I can close my eyes and experience again the flood of energy rising in me, a tornado of swirling feelings containing psychic debris for which I still have no labels. I began screaming in rage, rage at my sense of failure, rage at my helplessness before the forces of nature, rage for being a bad boy. I have but small sense of my mother in the memory. Only me. I was a bad boy. Shame on me. I cannot speak meaningfully of myself before that moment; it is my first memory, my first lasting impression of who I am, and in that sense I began then and there, in a whirlwind of emotions.

Religions know the importance of "In the beginning" stories. Most have them. These accounts vary from religion to religion but each has the task of instructing the faithful about who and what they are, where they belong, and how they ought to be in the world. It's little different with individuals. We each have our in-the-beginning accounts which seem to anticipate us. Some are about ancestors who by some accomplishment or bent of personality set the standard for the family, a yardstick by which all who follow are measured. Thankfully, most models are more vague than that, a We-Johnsons-are-a-stubborn-lot-but-we-always-accomplish-what-we-set-out-to-do kind of thing. Where it comes from no one knows, but every Johnson is touched by it nonetheless.

Not everyone is so blessed or cursed, of course. I never thought I was until my dad closed up his home of forty-odd years, and we children helped sort through the boxes of memories. In the process, a photo fell to my keeping, a picture of my Uncle *Bus* embracing my cousins Earl and Lorraine. Bus sports an indescribable hair disarrangement and is dressed in coarse, bibbed overalls. He sits on a wooden box before a weary, unpainted, house.

My cousin Earl looks to be about three years old. He clutches a ball, and wears a cap that belongs to someone in an *Our Gang* movie. I never knew Earl. He was an older cousin, became a minister, and lived out his life in Illinois.

Lorraine of the warm, pleasant features, then as now, has on those heavy stockings common to the time. They are rolled down to just below her chubby, year-and-a-half old knees. She seems to be offering a cookie to the photographer, probably her dad who appears in few of the old, family pictures simply because he was the family photographer. He died too young and I hold only the vaguest memories of him.

He took the photograph years before I was born, and yet the moment I identified it I experienced it as a part of my story, an explanation, in measure, of who I am, a parable of who I choose to be. Involved are blood-lines, but more so, values. Uncles and cousins, but also what they symbolize. What I get from the picture, I realize, comes from within me.

I see my uncle Bus enfolding in his strong arms the vulnerability and loveliness of children, assuring them that this is an okay and safe world to be in. I sense sturdiness and stability, an environment not needlessly complicated with the shadow of the Joneses. A world that honors hard work and provides unpretentious good times. And it's irrelevant whether or not this actually described my uncle, because for me it sets forth our family myth, the basics upon which our family, my mom and dad's family, was built. I never heard it articulated, but the photograph suddenly expressed it, and I recognized a spiritual, family portrait. None of my immediate family were portrayed, but it was a picture of us nonetheless. Composed from a collage of memories.

Uncle Bus and cousins

Memories are curious, powerful, possessions. They exist without boundaries. Sifted from time, they embrace more than time. Made up largely of shared experiences, they keep warm even that which never was shared. They are part projection composed of a multitude of life-forming conclusions, unconsciously splashed onto the canvas of the past. A few are but convenient concoctions that took on life. They draw nourishment from the stories we repeatedly heard of our parents, our siblings, and even ourselves. They provide background for the foreground of our own personal stories, which they subtly, and not so subtly, influence. Though often rearranged over time these creations are as essential to our being as those "true" memories that we insist are as clear and flawless as a cloudless, summer sky.

Play with your memories. They reveal your "self" much as do dreams. Do you know your first memory? Why it is your first? Why did you allow this memory to take root while other happenings of the time did not? What does your collection of early memories tell you about who you are today? If you have not taken time to walk that path, I encourage you to do so.

We remember for a reason. The stories we forget are legion, those that help explain who and what we are, we retain. It makes little difference how truly authentic they are, they reveal us nonetheless. We often unconsciously enrich memories with detail to make them "more accurate," convinced they are true snippets of past events. That's okay. They still provide us with a sense of our past and ourselves that we can have in no other way. And of early memories, first memories are the best, the first stone laid in the foundation of self.

My first memory is filled with infantile rage, mostly at myself. Also frustration and a sense of uncleanness. All are familiar to me. Rage is too strong a word, however. Anger is better. Anger is one of the ways I react to the world. Anger at those who exercise the power to take life from other beings, anger at the rapist, anger at those–as Oscar Wilde phrased it–"who know the price of everything, and the value of nothing," individuals so blinded by greed that they do not care the price paid by others for their actions; anger at war-makers, anger at the macho attitudes of many of my gender who, like dancing prairie chickens, believe they must continually authenticate themselves by displays of exaggerated "maleness." So many of this world's problems stem from this juvenile bent.

This surging reservoir provides a ready source of energy from which I often draw. I bleed it off in mostly productive ways. Much of my writing stems from the anger, though because I was well taught not to be an angry person, it sometimes comes out sideways. I'm usually aware when that happens.

A paradox of my life is that I have the anger, but not the permission to be angry, not overtly, at least. It took me almost a half-century to begin to express anger, but generally, it is not me. When I was small and would get foot-stomping mad my family would laugh me out of the tantrum. No matter how upset I became, they would discount my feelings by getting me to laugh. Consequently, I learned that if I wanted to be taken seriously, it could not be done through anger. Anger became the avenue of weakness and failure, an emotion I set aside or discounted as a liability for much of my life. It's ingenious how little people adapt and learn to cope.

Still, the anger in that first memory is familiar, so, too, the feeling of shame and uncleanness. By means, some so subtle that I cannot identify them, I learned that the body was "dirty." Disgrace was the body's shadow, and it followed everywhere. More generally, shaming was the primary tool my mother used to mold me into a presentable little boy. She worked at that. Each night as we knelt together at my bed and I offered the "Now I lay be down to sleep" prayer on which so many of us were raised, I was taught to end the supplication with petitions of blessings for all my loved ones, working from daddy and mommy down through my brother and three sisters, . . ."and God bless Shirley," and then the final appeal, or was it a plea, . . . "And help make me a good boy."

That was a long time ago and I'm not now sure whether the prayer was "help make me a better boy," or "help make me a good boy." The differences seem slight but they do suggest two different questions. Was I already good but just not yet at my pinnacle? Or was I in need of a real conversion from bad to good? Or was that just a standard book-prayer, one young mothers everywhere taught their little ones? Whatever the exact prayer, the method for making me a good, little boy was constant love, punctuated with occasional doses of shame. I thrived on the love. I don't remember ever feeling unloved, AND those moments of shaming painfully reminded me of my imperfections. Like all little ones, I simply did not question any pronouncement on the matter. I had done something shameful. Shame on me. And how I hated disappointing my parents.

In spite of its considerable formative power, I do not recommend shaming as a child-rearing tool. I'm two-thirds of a century removed from those early years of training and I still can be stopped in my tracks with an unanticipated, well-timed "ought" or "should." Caught off guard I easily flounder before people's expectations; I panic and whatever capabilities I have go dead in the grip of irrational fear; what I do will not measure up and I will disappoint others and shame myself. My own, private, little demon who has successfully resisted my best efforts at exorcism, though I have landed enough crippling blows that, with vigilance, I can keep him off balance.

My mother tried a few other tricks to civilize me, but compared to the shaming process, they were quite ineffective. I remember well a summer afternoon of my fourth year of life (it was spring in the McCurdy House so I would have been three-and-a-half). My prayers had not yet been fully answered and I remained shy a few credits of being a good boy. In mid-tantrum, I ran out the door and assumed a determined position under the big elm tree. My mother's friends from up the block came out and told me my mother had run away because I was being bad. My reaction is crystal clear in my memory. "Dumb big people. How stupid do you two think I am? My mother would never run away from me. She loves me. She would never leave me." That was beyond question. That was the strength of my assurance. I went in search of her, knowing she was hiding somewhere in the house, and that this was just a silly, little adult game to pull me into line. How often and how completely we can underestimate children.

Children have this wonderful grasp on important truth. My own three-year-old taught me this one summer afternoon at a lakeside family reunion. The air was hot and steamy, the gnats determined, and I was moody. My three-year-old held to the end of my arm like sticky candy, and I needed to wash. Finally, with considerable irritation I said, "Phillip, will you please let go of my hand." He looked up at me and said, "Why? You're my daddy." God could not have phrased it any better. I was reformed on the spot.

So it was that spring day in Pipestone. I had no doubt about the essential, loving nature of my world, and the neighbors' claim of my abandonment was without effect. Not so with the shaming. It took root and produced a hundred-fold.

I do not remember my dad ever shaming me, but, as I said, it was a tool of my mother's, and my four, older siblings often took up the practice. I suffered without recourse at the bottom of a substantial pecking order.

The shaming process possesses several telling elements. First, it comes from above. Most always from people bigger, stronger and wiser. Curiously, this never attached itself to my concept of God. Shame never became part of my religious understanding. Though some people authoritatively offered me the poisonous potion of guilt, and then the religious antidote, forgiveness, I never could swallow it. Building a religious identity out of being woefully unacceptable to a loving "Father" whose anger had to be bought off by the excruciating suffering of one without guilt never made sense to me, largely because I knew my own dad was above such outrageous behavior. Sadly, in those days the most dogmatic branches of the Church offered no alternative understandings on the matter. Paradoxically, I never doubted God's love for all of us, AND the effects of shaming on me could not have been more substantial had God spoken the words and shaved the Divine finger. We truly can compartmentalize our lives.

That, of course, is the second part of the process. Along with coming from "above," there is the finger pointing right at you. At lonely you. Behind the finger is a wrinkled face, always furrowed with emotion.

Then the drawing of one index finger down the other index finger. I never knew what that signified, but it had the effect of showering me with my shame like the shavings from a whittled stick.

And there were the intoned words. In a good shaming they were delivered in cadence with the stroked finger. Sometimes the *shame* was emphasized, sometimes the *you*. I maintained a clear preference for the shame. "SHAME on you" was a bit less lethal than "Shame on YOU." Either way, it was not comfortable for a three or four-year-old. The absolute worst possibility in a shaming was when the face and the tone of voice teamed up in an expression of disgust and revulsion, like the speaker didn't even want to be in the same room with me because I was so revolting. Indeed, that was part of the feeling that accompanied my first memory, a general feeling of unwelcomeness. In subsequent years the feeling attached itself to cold sores.

Painful, unsightly cold sores frequently afflicted me during my early years, and in response my dad offered me his only bad piece of advice, a bit of Kentucky lore. "Rub the cold sore three times with your finger, and then rub your finger behind your ear." Though done repeatedly, it never worked. I would ponder whether I was to give the sore three, precise strokes and then transfer it to behind the ear, or whether I was to rub it three different times, going to the ear after each excoriation. Like the seeker after Divine healing who determines that the lack of results comes from a lack of faith, I believed that the process failed because I did not do it exactly right. But so desperate was I to initiate a cure, that I tried it in every conceivable combination throughout my grade-school years. I would rub so long and hard that I thought I could surely erase the vile thing completely. That, of course, only irritated and spread the sores. I would have the unsightly things halfway around my mouth, and feelings of uncleanness always accompanied them. How I hated the loathsome things. Cold sores no longer plague me, but for years into young adulthood, an emerging blister would make me feel grimy from head to toe. My entire body participated in the uncleanness.

Just before my high school Skip Day trip I developed the granddaddy of all cold sores. I was seventeen, anticipating a free and fun-filled day, and woke up that morning a Frankenstein monster. An unsightly blister filled the space between my upper lip and my nose. I told several people that I had burned myself trying to light a cigarette with a blow torch. The angry wound from a burn would be ugly, but it would not be "unclean." I would not be unclean. I could lie to others, of course, but not to myself. The day slowly filled with unspoken rage over my self-betrayal. I became brother to those leprous souls of Biblical times who had to stay off the beaten path and warn every one of their despicable presence with shouts of "Unclean! Unclean!" Only in the late night darkness of the bus trip back home, when Joan Breuer, Roger Wood, and I clustered up to tell naughty stories, did I experience some relief. The darkness was a friend, the dirty stories a cleansing.

Most of my early memories are good, of course. For instance, in my very first memory of my dad, he carries me through the floodwaters surrounding the McCurdy House, to the uncomplaining Whippet standing hub-deep in water up the street. I retain no sense of the import of the family home being surrounded by water. I recollect no sense of impending danger, presumably because there was none. Only of my dad stepping into the back wash room of our home wearing funny boots. I don't even remember what the boots looked like, only that they were different, something I had never seen before. I now assume they were hip boots. He picked me up and safely carried me to the waiting car. I still can replay the feeling of being secure in his arms. What my memory might be had he slipped and fallen into the water I can only imagine, but he didn't, because he was my daddy. Such is the way things get filed away in memory. This is the first memory I can give a date to, and therefore a precise age to. The floodwaters that broke out of the banks of the Dredge, the raging waters that carried eight hapless Holsteins from the pasture across the road and hurled them to their deaths on the rocks at the bottom of Winnewissa Falls, resulted from a two-day downpour on June 28 and 29, 1938. I was three-years-seven-months old.

Early memories carry much baggage. In sharing just three of my own I have revealed more about myself than I might choose to do in other ways. It's a bit scary not knowing what the reader might do with the stories, perhaps drawing conclusions that go beyond the realities, perhaps because I have over dramatized them. So, this is an exercise in trust. Whatever. Such early recollections are peek-holes into our souls. Again, I encourage you to look closely at your own. Much of who and what you are is encapsulated there.

The five of us: Doris Elaine, Kenneth Virgil, Shirley
Ardell, Betty Jean, and in front, Richard Allan.

Chapter Four and One Half

The Spittoon

From the time I was three-and-a-half years old my brother Kenny took me to the movies. Admission for him was ten cents. Because he held me on his lap I was admitted free, although he now confesses that in the darkness of the theater he would sometimes put me in the adjacent seat.

The trip to the State Theater required a seven-block walk up Second Avenue, past the Armour Plant, and across five or six railroad tracks. Through all my years of growing up and over many treks to town, this last stretch always provided the most interest. It was short on lighting and long on oil tanks, boxcars, grain elevators, warehouses, and shadows. Somehow a big cottonwood tree had taken root and had been allowed to be, and it, of course, would rustle in the breeze. When I was old enough to make the trip alone this was always the scariest part, and when with friends, the most fun.

Our town boasted two theaters, the *Orpheum* and the *Alo*, later renamed the *State*. The State ran mostly two reelers, often double-features, and my early view of the world was formed, in part, in its hard, straight-backed seats. Jane Withers, the Dead-End Kids, the Durango Kid, and Johnny Mac Brown were my mentors.

One night a scruffy, old miner in a "Western" introduced me to the marvelous world of spittoons. While everyone else was absorbed in such plot as the movie afforded, I was captivated by the shiny, brass container into which he repeatedly spewed marvelous streams of tobacco juice. I could hardly wait to get home to duplicate this astounding, physical feat.

The next day I played cowboy. Not shoot-em-up or galloping-around cowboy, but the in-the-bar version. It was a chilly, overcast day and I wore both coat and cap, gear a bit out of character for cowboying, but I did the best I could. The warmest place out of the wind was on the back porch. That became my saloon.

Mom provided me with an empty, one-pound, coffee can, which I set by the steps. I then busied myself with indoor cowboy activities, which consisted mostly of cowboy talk, cowboy swagger, and repeated strides past my spittoon. With each passing I spat at the can. It was important to do it from a distance, like in the movie; indeed, that was the wondrous beauty of the act. I played for some time and spit myself dry, but never could I produce anything resembling the stream of juice produced by the old miner, and after my best sustained effort I had not even wet the bottom of the can. I finally gave up, frustrated with being small.

It would be years before I learned the role tobacco played in the miner's achievement, and more years still before I discovered that spittoons are half-filled with water to make them easier to clean (someone actually has to do that). Although I still occasionally spit, I never have had another go at a spittoon.

Chapter Five

....

Reflections of Eden

On the Mountains of the Prairie,
On the great Red Pipe-stone Quarry,
Gitche Manito, the mighty,
He the Master of Life, descending,
On the red crags of the quarry
Stood erect, and called the nations,
Called the tribes of men together.
H. W. Longfellow

In March of 1938 we moved 150 yards to the Johnson house, the last
one on Hiawatha Avenue and the only one situated north of Quarry Road
(Moving in March was a carryover from earlier times when March was the
first month of the year, and the time to start new ventures and transact
new business). We trucked and trailered our possessions from the friendly,
four-room, fixture-begging McCurdy house, around the corner to the
two-storied affair with its huge, gravity furnace, its kitchen faucet, which
pumped water up from the basement cistern, and its sympathetically
shorter trek to the outhouse. This new home offered more bedrooms than
we had beds. Clearly we were moving up, even though we migrated from
the last house on Second Avenue to the last house on Hiawatha Avenue.
We were the ultimate Northenders.

Most people have read that the first three years of life forms our personalities, our values, and perspectives. For better or worse, that took place

for me in the McCurdy house. But it was when we moved to the Johnson house that my life began expanding, and in ways that speak of blessings all around. You see, and I'm playing a bit–I love to play–I was raised near the east gate of the *Garden of Eden*.

Barely three hundred yards from the front door of that house, the *Great Spirit* once called the warring Indian Nations together. In their presence he broke off a piece of the flesh-colored ledge upon which he stood and in his mighty hands molded a calumet. Holding it high above the peoples, he turned it to the north and to the south, to the east and to the west and told them that the soft, red stone was the flesh of their ancestors, that it belonged to all tribes, and that neither threat nor war club was again to be raised on the sacred ground that held the stone.

That explains our fruitless childhood searches for arrowheads. The Native Americans faithfully followed the Great Spirit's command and his call for peace. Pilgrims from a variety of Indian Nations traveled weeks to quarry the sacred stone, but at some distance from the site they would break their arrows and discard their bows before entering the scared land. When early White settlers learned the significance of this special location they used it to stimulate tourist traffic, scandalously promoting the site as the, "Indian's Garden of Eden." The claim stuck, and I grew up with that understanding.

Because the Indians fiercely defended this sacred site, the settlers did not enter the area until the 1870's. Once there, however, they ignored the Indians' sensitivities, gobbling up the land and quickly turning the inviolate soil. In a short generation the children of the Garden's defenders were reduced to working the White man's quarries, wresting red quartzite from the ledge, ironically to build, among other things, the invader's halls of justice. In spite of the gross infringement, the Great Spirit patiently lingered, and in time peace returned to the land. Under that blessing of peace we lived.

The Johnson house faced west across the tar road to the rock-strewn pastureland where the Indian School's *Aberdeen Angus* grazed, each black cow a carbon copy of every other one. Beyond that, balanced on the horizon, lay the Rock Island railroad tracks, carefully stitched together by Chinese work crews of an earlier time. Five blocks south where the North End began, the tracks intersected with Hiawatha, but then curved gracefully past the depot until they tracked due north, paralleling the tar road all the way to the Indian School and enchantingly beyond.

Twice that first Spring mother, most certainly driven by my whining about having nothing to do, took me to the tracks. Together we laid straight pins on the rail, stretched a strip of cloth over them and anchored the cloth at both ends with rocks. Then we waited for the approaching train. As it slowly groaned and creaked by the engineer waved, believing, I'm, sure, that we stood there to admire his great charge, but no, we were waiting for its awesome bulk to flatten our pins into swords, swords so little I could find no meaningful way to play with them; they didn't even have handles. On one of her bad days my next older sister was taken to the tracks to make blades for little scissors (each of us being groomed for our roles in life). Her results were as unsatisfying as mine, but at least mom tried. She must have caught on though, for I remember only two such excursions.

Beyond the tracks the land sloped from sight to rise into view again a half-mile west. The unseen hollow between cradled the Garden of Eden and the line of quarries from which Native Americans still harvest the soft, red stone. In bygone years it was to this place that Dakota and Fox, Ojibwe and Cheyenne and Sak came to harvest the unique stone (Catlinite), officially named after George Catlin, the first White man to visit the area in 1835. How inappropriate that the stone, so sacred to the Native Americans, should officially bare the name of a White intruder. The winners, as we know, always write the history. It was also to this sacred site that Chief Inkpaduta and his band came with their White prisoners following the Spirit Lake Massacre in 1857.

From the railroad tracks we could see the huge, granite boulders mischievously left behind by the last, chuckling glacier. Called the "Three Maidens," these startlingly out-of-place giants were actually five in number, seeping water and groaning ice having split and increased their numbers over time. Everyone from the area climbed and scampered over these monsters, and leaping rock to rock was a rite of passage for the young. According to Indian legend two old women had been carried to beneath the rocks in a blaze of fire to act as guardian spirits of the quarries. Before harvesting the stone one needed first to propitiate these spiritual custodians.

Moving north along the east rim of the "garden" the scattered quartzite rock jutting up through the virgin prairie became increasingly conspicuous and noticeably more tormented to become a complex stonescape that slowly reached higher and higher, at last taking on real authority, at least by prairie standards, to become a genuine meandering precipice. Unforgiving boulders by the hundreds lay strewn among the scrub oak below the cliff. Through the eyes of parents it was a place filled with hazard for small children. To children, it was a romantic place laced with challenge. Here the Dredge had been channeled by early engineers to tumble over the stone ledge as Winnewissa Falls. In flood time its cascading, rush of water could be spectacular, the roar of it discernible all the way to our house. We children proved ourselves by leaping from rock to rock to cross the creek at the base of the falls. Admittedly it was a "low water" activity, but one each in their turn undertook.

Not far from the falls the somber "stone face" cast a steady gaze over the area. The face-like profile constituted one facet of a stone column known as "leaping rock." Allegedly the Native Americans would make its already smooth surface even more treacherous by smearing it with buffalo fat. To prove their manhood young men would leap to the small area atop the column and plant an arrow in a crevice. As I recall, the chasm spanned about thirteen feet, no mean distance in itself, but made more challenging because the terrain provided no opportunity for a decent running start. Around the base of the column lay a confusion of threatening boulders. If the legends were true the leap indeed offered challenge, but also the risk of severe injury or death if one failed.

From the north one could step across a much smaller space to plant feet on the column, but to my knowledge no one from my era ever attempted the manhood-proving test from the east. Not even Virgil (see below). In the late forties the Federal Park Service assigned Lyle Lynch to oversee what had been designated a National Shrine, and he cleared out the tumble of boulders beneath leaping rock, perhaps in fear that sooner or later the requisite fool would appear and attempt the leap.

The "Falls," as the entire area was known, was a cornucopia of curiosities. For instance, one could visit the track of the great Thunderbird who had delivered the young, virgin survivor of the primeval flood, from the precipice to safety on a hill in the far West. Also, in 1838 a geographical survey team, under the leadership of Joseph Nicollet, left their "tracks," chiseling into the hard Sioux Quartzite the record of their passing. Even the creeping ice-pack of the glacial age left its calling card: deep scratches in the stone, in two directions. Curiously, the same glacier carved out no lakes in the county.

The Falls boasted a cave-of-sorts, really little more than a deep fissure in the cliff. We would periodically work our way into its always cool interior, but also would gather our numbers before its opening to yell, "What are you doing in there?", convincing ourselves that the resulting reverberations said, "Nothing."

In my time "silver spoon tree" shaded a small area above the falls. It may still be there, though I doubt the silver spoon that gave the tree its name is still visible. Some pioneer picnicker had attached a spoon to the tree and slowly the tree was overgrowing it. Part of the spoon handle still was visible through an annually shrinking hole, and those with small fingers would reach in and touch it "for good luck."

In the paintings made by the earliest White explorers the area was bereft of trees, but in the interim scrub oak had taken root in every hospitable and not so hospitable place. Indeed, one could walk most of the trails, always in shade. "The Falls" constituted our summertime play ground, and when we were older, a place we would visit at night to play a game we called, "drag net." I was the proud "inventor" of this game where one person placed themselves at the base of the cliff while the others formed a half-circle around him at some distance from the wall. Then slowly the ring would be tightened and the challenge for the person who was "it" was to sneak out unseen and untouched. With so many avenues to crawl along and recesses in which to hide, it was not all that hard to slip by undetected.

Closer to home than the Falls were two abandoned quarries, the "wet" one and the "dry" one. These lay to the south of the Three Maidens. Although I still remember the roar of the quarriers' stonecutter, it fell silent about the time we moved to Hiawatha Avenue. By the time I was old enough to play around the quarries all that remained of the quarrying operation was a huge pile of red stone dust. Much of it had washed over the east quarry wall to create a red sand beach, a favorite swimming area for the young. At the bottom of the quarry, about twelve feet at its deepest, you could still see the rails and an abandoned handcart of that earlier era.

The wet quarry was spring fed, and I suspect the determined, underground waters led to the early closing down of the work there, though I don't know that to be true. The dry quarry lay immediately south and has since been filled in, but in those days it was a favorite playground. Rainwater would collect in various pools there, and at least one was large enough and deep enough to be a swimming pool for us all summer long. Indeed, we once built a raft from which we could dive into its warm waters. The quarry had been abandoned so long before that towering cottonwood trees grew within its bounds. We sometimes pitched our sleeping blankets beneath them for an overnight camp out. The quarry also was a place to catch frogs and garter snakes, and in the winter to careen down its snow covered cliffs on cardboard sleds. Surprisingly, no one ever broke his neck.

It was on an island of quarry scraps that I made an intriguing find one day. I was sitting on a large slab of rock picking up and tossing smaller chunks into the water. In the process I unearthed a metal, first aid kit, its seams carefully taped over to keep out the water. Inside was a collection of tokens and three, gold, pocket watch, cases. Tokens had ceased to be "legal tender" in town and how long the box had lain there I can only guess. I suspect the one who put it there could not find the spot again to recover the contents, and how improbable that any one should come upon it. But I did. Because my friend Roger was close at hand and helped to dig it out of its crevice, we lay joint claim to it. We use to keep it hidden under the crawl space beneath the Gist kitchen. Whatever became of it, I have no idea.

This grand playground of creek and Falls and quarry we north-enders considered ours. This was our territory. Our claim was pure fantasy, of course, as people from both south of the tracks and from the Indian School freely roamed the same area, and had we tried to keep them out we would have failed miserably; we controlled nothing. Still, we had the easiest access to it, and it felt like ours, and for us it substituted for the swimming pool and playgrounds and ball fields of the town on the other side of the tracks.

Still, territorial boundaries did exist between we and the Indian students. For instance, their Saturday treks into town for the 2:00 o'clock matinee at the Orpheum ran through "our" territory. Week by week we threw down the gauntlet before them. They greatly outnumbered us, but in winter we built snow forts along the tar road and stockpiled snow balls, showering them with our ammunition and challenging them to "come and get us." In summer the snowballs became green apples, green tomatoes, and on occasion, mud balls. They often ignored our generally ineffectual attacks, and on other occasions returned the fire. When they marshaled their forces and stormed our fortifications we would shamelessly scatter into the sanctuary of neighborhood yards. The lawns and gardens were indisputable non-Indian space, an area the students never stepped into. It was fairly innocent fun, because once they moved on up Hiawatha we would follow them to town for the matinee.

The Indians' generally unchallenged territory, "theirs" because of its proximity to the school, lay north of The Falls. Here sprawled the school dump and the rock-studded pasture land where the school's Holstein dairy herd and huge draft horses grazed.

Our Boy Scout troop once ventured into this space on a winter hike. Our fearless scoutmaster led us along the railroad tracks to just north of the reservation campus where we settled among the rocks and started fires for our aluminum foil dinners. After we ate, the leader went farther out into the prairie with a scout to work on some merit badge requirements. The rest of us relaxed by the fire, swapping stories until Harold interrupted. "Holy Jesus!" he said, pointing. We all looked in the direction of his outstretched arm.

Uniformly rising as one over the crest of the hill, evenly strung out for over a city block, came forty to fifty Indian students, the blood of ancestor warriors pulsing through their veins. Chippewa, Sauk, and Fox, all aligned in a united front against the White intruders. It was their consummate moment, exquisitely executed, and even in my immediate uncertainty I felt a spurt of envy. They advanced toward us at an unhurried but steady pace, confidently swinging the line around to cut off our retreat towards town. In all our jostlings with the Indian students no real animosity had ever built; ours was a relationship of competition. But this was different, dramatically so. And unprecedented. Believing we were in for a beating, we scurried among the rocks like chipmunks, gathering up our gear. When Roger picked up his hatchet and pulled off the sheaf a chilling fear rippled through me; I was afraid he might use it.

Then a beautiful, terrible, tragic thing happened. Our scoutmaster saw the war party and came running up the hill, canteen banging, banging, banging on his knee. The man stood about 5'6", which made him shorter than some of the scouts and many of the Indian boys, but he was an adult, and it made all the difference in the world. I can only guess at the Indian experience but suspect the same training that made a sanctuary of our yards also took effect on that snow-laced hillside, an injunction that thundered, DON'T MESS WITH WHITE AUTHORITY. Whatever the roots of the sweet calamity, the rank of advancing warriors broke and as one hightailed it back over the hill towards the school, their precious moment of glory dissipated in unearned ignominy before the charge of one plump and aging scoutmaster. He was Pharaoh; they were the oppressed standing in need of a Moses.

I became acquainted with the Indian School in 1939. On Thursday evenings the neighborhood kids would band together and walk to the school to see a free movie. To my knowledge no one from south of the tracks ever attended; this was a carefully guarded "North End" thing. Beginning that first summer in the Johnson House I was allowed to join the group.

Just beyond the halfway point to the school a bridge spanned the Dredge. It was a concrete affair with cement pillars and an iron railing. The railing included a series of rings, which were just large enough to stick your head through so you could spit into the flowing water below. Although the older kids refrained from such childish behavior, for we younger ones this was a ritual of the trip. These outings were grand adventures.

The walk home along the unlighted road was more exciting still. The rustling cottonwood trees at the bridge and the voiceless dark of prairie on both sides of the road quickened our imaginations. What a precious gift of childhood—knowing threat without substance, fear without danger. We would dare one another to walk into the gloom of the deep ditch, and sometimes, secure in our numbers, form a tight little circle there to tell ghost stories. Occasionally, the Black Angus would startle us with their presence and we would shriek and run through the night, savoring the ecstasy of shared fright and flight.

About the time we moved into the Johnson house, I started Sunday School. This was preceded by my baptism, which took place in our living room instead of the church, because my mother was afraid that when the good reverend put water on my head I would call him a jackass, my favorite word at the time. Mom worried about such things. Indeed, our family crest carried the motto, "What will the neighbors think?" How curious that that question would even be considered, given the time and place.

With one or two exceptions, our neighbors were glaringly unpretentious, and but for the household cats, not an aristocrat lived among us. We were a community of people who never made the "Personal Mention" column in the *County Star,* who gratefully complimented our assorted dinner ware with the cups, bowls, and saucers that came secreted in the cardboard cylinders of oat meal, and who thought dribbling *Karo* corn syrup over our pancakes was the way of the world.

One notable exception to this was "grandma Beck," an enlightened lady who kept sugar cubes in her kitchen for visiting youngsters. "Grandma" was short, with a pleasant face that wrinkled up in the middle of a laugh. Her bright, south-facing kitchen was a warm sanctuary on a cold winter day, and I visited it more than once with mom. It contained things our modest kitchen did not have, and especially one device I absolutely coveted. You could actually place a peeled, hard-boiled egg onto a little cradle and with one stroke of a lever, cut the egg into wonderful, gold and white slices. I tell you, it was a marvel.

Mom certainly wanted the Becks to think well of us, but why she worried about the others is curious. For instance, one of the more interesting couples in the neighborhood on occasion took their problems on tour. Physically. One Sunday morning, after we had moved again, this time into the Gist house, this couple wound up in our back yard with a healthy entourage of unabashed onlookers. The wife was after the husband who did everything he could to avoid her. She would run him down, throw a sweeping haymaker to his jaw, and he would go sprawling, then crawling in his futile attempt to escape her fury. This was great theatre, and I did not understand that the husband was falling-down drunk, which occasioned the fight. When the ruckus moved on, the younger Gist kids shamelessly followed. In time the fight concluded in the couple's own back yard. In the only offensive move I saw him attempt, the man stepped forward to swing at his wife. As he did so he stepped on a beer bottle, lost his balance, and went down like a sack of potatoes, with her all over him. At that point discretion overcame curiosity (either that or we recognized that the fight was over) and I was ushered home. Mom worried about how these people viewed her family though.

So, too, with the scandal of the neighborhood, a man and woman who lived together without benefit of clergy. No one knew how to relate to people living in such blatant sin, and they were generally avoided. Years later when I became the couple's paper boy I discovered they were decent people, something dad had quietly maintained all along. That was fortunate, for mom worried how they might view us.

In truth, the people in our neighborhood were too close to the earth to look down on anyone. For instance, earlier in the depression some of the neighborhood men would walk the railroad tracks, five-gallon buckets in hand, picking up the occasional piece of coal that had fallen from the loco-motive tender. The coal was a precious commodity, burning longer and hotter than the wood that generally fueled most space heaters. Actually, the Gists burned a lot of cobs; we always had a large pile of them in the back yard. Anyway, everyone knew that one year this one neighbor managed to steal the buckets of coal from at least two of his neighbors. He typically was viewed as shady. As a teenager I learned to know this man as one who worked at filing false claims with his insurance company. My sisters knew him as the lecher who tried to get kisses from them every time he escorted them home from babysitting his son. They never told my parents about this, however, and he remained one of those whose opinions mattered.

We also sported a self-proclaimed atheist, a soured, lonely, old man who didn't need the support of God to attack others. Stubbornness and rancor were in his genes. His front gate always was locked, his lawn perpetually unmowed. If he ever ventured beyond his yard I never saw it happen, though he was often at the fence ready to do battle. In a town served only by the *Minneapolis* (evening) *Star* and (morning) *Tribune* he somehow managed to read "The only fit paper in the State," the *St. Paul Pioneer Press.* I learned this one Saturday when I called on him to see if he would be interested in subscribing to a Minneapolis daily for 12 weeks. (I was working for some prize offered by the Tribune, but the North End never was a productive area when searching out new subscribers. Over the years I never won anything.)

This prickly man took the same kind of pride in his atheism as the rest of us did in our denominational affiliations. As kids we often spoke of the special virtues of being Methodist, Catholic, Baptist, or as I was, Evangelical, comparing buildings (ours was small enough to fit into the basement of the Methodist Church), or preachers (Evangelicals had good ones), or sometimes beliefs. We Protestants counted ours, the Catholic kids proudly weighed theirs. The Baptists, of course, were the only ones who baptized according to the Bible.

Which god or gods our atheist neighbor discarded I never knew, though I suspect his list was shorter than mine became. He always was ready to argue with whomever talked with him, but he could hardly argue with God, for then he would have had to acknowledge God. To his credit, he basked in the luxury of his sure belief system, unlike me, who finds too many bones to pick with God to insure our relationship. In addition to his denial of an Almighty, this man was cheap, the kind of person who would change his name so he could save a few coins on a used tomb stone. But gosh, mom did not want him thinking poorly of us.

The North End also harbored those who tranquilized their unshared pain with alcohol. For instance, every Saturday night one diminutive couple dressed up in their best "go-to-meetin" duds, he in black suit and tie, she in a floor-length black dress with a narrow, white collar. Soaking wet and together they could not have tipped the scales at two-hundred pounds. They would get drunk in the *Friendly Bar* and then adjourn to the sidewalk out front to dance. They were totally harmless and probably needed the dance. Routinely the police would take them to jail and they would emerge Sunday morning to disappear from sight for another week. They were charming in their own way, or maybe their doll-like size made them seem so. When I was fourteen my dad and I found the woman face down in a snow bank in sub-zero weather one Saturday night. By this time she was a widow, but carrying on as best she could in her husband's absence.

I received an occasional spanking while growing up, with one especially well-deserved, though humiliating, episode coming in front of my friends after I told my mother to "Shut up!" I was about nine at the time. But the parents of four of my friends did their "instructing" with lengths of garden hose, belts, and even clubs, a practice my parents abhorred. Also, there were the children of several families my mother didn't like me playing with because they were really bad and she was afraid they would lead me into trouble. Yet, she worried over what these families might think of we Gists.

You get the idea. Mom couldn't help herself. She probably had OCD (I had to get it from someplace), but we wouldn't have known it at the time. Whatever, no one's opinion mattered more than the preacher's, so Mom's concern led her to ask for a home baptism, and her request was honored. I don't know if she honestly explained the situation to the good, *Rev. Minor P. Northem*, later to become my brother's father-in-law, but on the morning of Wednesday, April 5th, 1939, he and his wife came to the house for the event. I still remember him sitting in the horsehair, easy chair in our living room and gently pulling me around the left arm to speak somber words while he sprinkled water on my head. My silence throughout did my mother proud, and I officially became a member of the Body of Christ.

Our living room was probably the best place for the cleansing Sacrament to be administered because that was the very room of my most sordid sin up to that time. 1939 was the year I became aware of feminine beauty. My sisters had a friend, Eunice, who I thought was the most desirable female on earth. I remember longing to be included in the fun around the dining room space heater one cold winter day, and realized I wanted her to kiss me. My older brother and I were ever so briefly rivals for her attention, and I lost. I don't remember whether it was on the rebound or not, or which event preceded the other, but I also fell in love with a beautiful woman with feathers. She was dressed all in white, had this beautiful face, and stood caringly over two small children at a small footbridge that spanned a stream of clear water. I spent much time admiring this winged woman who resided in our hallway calendar.

The footbridge reminded me both of the place where *Billy Goat Gruff* encountered the troll, and the bridge the selfish little dog trotted over when he spotted his own reflection in the water and lost his bone as he greedily barked for the other. The latter seemed to be my mother's favorite morality tale and I heard it repeatedly in the Johnson House. If I was growing into a selfish, greedy child, I'm not aware of it, but it seemed to be a primary concern of hers.

Anyway, several times in the permissiveness of an empty downstairs I took the calendar from the wall and snuck it behind the davenport. The couch sat diagonally in one corner of the living room, and the space behind was my favorite retreat. There, in great secrecy, I worshiped the woman's beauty and discreetly planted kisses upon her.

The last time I made off with her I had to temporarily leave her unceremoniously scrunched beneath the davenport. Mother had come downstairs from her sewing to begin supper. I waited for the opportunity to climb a chair and return the angel to her place, but it never came. In the end I abandoned her on the floor beneath the nail, hoping people would believe she had accidentally fallen. Thus the foolish affair was brought to an undignified end.

Spring 1939 was also the season I gave up belief in the Easter Bunny. That Easter morning mom took me to the landing outside the kitchen door and pointed down the steps to the basement door of the house. A light snow had fallen over night, and there, leading right up to the door were the tracks of a rabbit. I quickly dressed and went to follow that fellow on his rounds. And indeed, he led me round and round, in the pastureland beyond the north fence. In time I lost his trail in the tangle of other rabbit tracks, and that morning lay aside the absurdity of a rabbit somehow carrying eggs and candy and depositing these in each of the houses in the neighborhood.

That next winter I also would wrestle with the whole Santa Claus thing, but with that I came out a believer. We had no fire place and I knew he could not get the furnace door open from the inside, and also that it was unbearably hot in that chamber, so I concluded that in cases like ours he simply used the door. That also would explain why no deer or sleigh tracks appeared on our roof; he obviously landed on the hard-packed driveway.

Unlike the Easter bunny, he was not yet to be doubted. After all, I had seen him (we very discretely exposed children to only one in those days), and he certainly snuck in with presents while we attended the Christmas Eve services at church. No, Santa was real in the Johnson house.

Like many in my generation I grew up on the powerful, intellectual food of nursery rhymes. What are little girls made of? And little boys? My literal understanding of the snails and puppy dog tails presented me with a curious and difficult to accommodate fact of life. The sugar and spice stuff was not so murky.

The claims of the nursery rhymes did not always hold true, however. Arland and Virgil were brothers, a year apart in age, from the same family, sharing a common bedroom, and yet they were the night and day, the Esau and Jacob of the neighborhood. Virgil was pure snail and puppy-dog tail; unadulterated tough. Had a circus of male attributes been put together, he would have held center ring. Every death-defying feat, every head-in-the-lion's-mouth spectacular would have featured Virgil. He was the only one from the neighborhood to dive from the very top of the ledge into the water of the quarry far below. Everyone else dove from a spot several feet lower, a place created by my brother Kenny and Bob Stolte. They worked most of an afternoon with crow bars to slowly lever a multi-ton rock out of the cliff to watch it splash into the water below. Virgil tore a fingernail off one day when his dive carried him too close to the submerged boulder. Such was typical. He was the fastest runner, the surest catcher, the highest jumper. His role in life was to be the leader in the art of being male. He didn't work at it. He just was it.

The last time I saw Virgil I was fourteen. My two best friends, Roger and John, brothers, and I were coming home from the late and memorable double feature at the State—*Law of the Timber* and *Killer Dill*. The snow made crunching sounds under our feet in the bitter cold as we hurried to be home by midnight. We were on the gravel road, and as we passed Diedrich's house we saw flames leaping from a house on Hiawatha. We sprang into action, sending John, the youngest, to the Beck house to wake them up to call the fire department. Roger and I ran through the yards to the burning house.

The husband and father of the family that lived there was running round in the snow, barefoot and in his underclothes, screaming and trying to find a way to get back into the building. The heat was too intense, and by the time the volunteer fire department arrived the situation was hopeless. Everything was made worse when the nearest fire hydrant produced no water. The firefighters had to string fire hose several blocks from somewhere south of the tracks. After a time Virgil and some of his friends arrived. Even though the interior of the house was a whirlwind of flame, with smoke and fire spewing out of every opening, with glass panes wilting from the heat, Virgil had to be wrestled from off the front porch by his friends. He already had pushed the front door open when they grabbed him. The woman inside was a product of the North End, someone he had played with and known all his life, and she and her baby were inside. It was clear to everyone present that no one could be alive in the building, and that entry was out of the question, but as his friends dragged him away and held him he pleaded with them to let him go, sobbing that that someone had to try. It was the most heroic thing I've ever witnessed. He would have tried. He did try.

Arland had the same athletic body of his brother, and may very well have possessed similar courage, but in every other way he was different. From Virgil. From other boys. He was composed of sugar and spice. Even as a five-year-old I became aware of the dissimilarity. For instance, Arland had a lilting voice that absolutely intrigued me. Nobody else talked like him. And Arland played with the girls.

One August afternoon my sisters sat in our front yard and wrapped their hair in strips of cloth to make pipe curls. Hey, I wanted pipe curls too. My hair was certainly too short for such but they made a big thing of twisting it in some rags, and I was satisfied. We then took a tour of the neighborhood to allow our hair to dry. When we got to the dirt road, the one connecting the tar road with the gravel road like a rung on the ladder (7th St.), we met Arland. He had on a long, black dress, black hat complete with veil, high heels, and rouge. He bustled along with his sister and two neighborhood girls who also were dressed for tea. And I stood there with rags in my hair and knew that Arland was different. Not different good, not different bad, just different.

My brother and sisters were more of an age with Arland and when I recently asked three of them about him, curiously, each used the same word to describe him. The word is not a part of my working vocabulary, and because all three used it, I assume it was the operative word of their youth. They classified Arland as the "sissified" one, a rather benign description in that it was not a nominalization. They didn't call him a sissy, only the one with the sissified manners.

That fits my memory. The young inhabitants of the Garden had not yet sampled the fruit of the forbidden tree, the fruit that so easily turns reality to illusion. None apparently knew the ugly words that give birth to uglier feelings, creating in our minds things not apparent to our eyes. In the peace of the Garden, Arland was Arland. And he was enough.

It was, indeed, an innocent age. I was twenty-one years old, almost four years in the military, and in northern Japan. One of my service buddies returned from leave in Tokyo. I shared a room with a young man from

Florida, and we sat with this third fellow as he described his R and R. He related being in a bar, seeing two, attractive young women, approaching them, only to discover they were Lesbians. My roommate and I looked at each other and shrugged. We had never heard the term before. When the third fellow explained I shrugged again and said I didn't know that such things happened. It was little more than a curiosity.

Several years ago I asked an older Northender if he knew what ever became of Arland. He said yes, and went on to describe him in the ugliest of homophobic terms. He did not describe Arland, however, but rather voiced a repugnance that had grown within himself, an ugliness absorbed from the worst parts of our world. H had learned the words that create illusion. The poor man had eaten from the forbidden tree, now seeing the world in terms of good and evil.

I've never been able to understand all that. Here I am, standing on the threshold of retirement. Yet, when I was in seminary the evidence that homosexual people just are, like Arland just was, was persuasive, and yet all these years later some people still will not let evidence interfere with their prejudices. Just this week my state representative made the newspapers as he took his stand against the homosexual community, which was "a threat to good family values and good families everywhere." I fail to understand how blind prejudice contributes to good family values. To this day I do not know if this child of God is homosexual, transsexual, or a transvestite, but whatever his constitution, in the eyes of some he stands condemned.

Many years ago I occasionally visited a gentle, timid, little old man in a nursing home. One day I asked him how he spent his time and he said "Reading my Bible and trying not to get angry." That put an ache in my stomach. Probing deeper I discovered that for him going to bed in the evening was an act filled with terror because he believed one night he would fall asleep and wake up in hell. Over a very long time I came to know the source of his fear; he was homosexual with a lifetime of instruction that he was a blight on society and an offense to God. Religion had robbed him of his life. That needs to be italicized: *Religion (and good family values) had robbed him of his life.* The only life God had given him. Religion is dangerous enough that people should be required to earn a license to practice it. And perhaps none should be issued.

Thankfully, the spiritual incubator of the North End taught its children none of the ugliness that my grandchildren are exposed to early and frequently. Indeed, if Arland, had not been older than I, he would have been a member in good standing in the most exclusive male club to which I've belonged. Actually, I'm not a joiner and have never been part of a "club," and the group I'm referring to never was designated as such, and it was far too small to have been considered a movement. From its beginning to its end it never numbered more than six or seven people, all boys, who routinely, nay, religiously, on their way home from the Orpheum Theatre at night, and upon crossing the Rock Island Rail Road tracks, would unzip their overalls, and while walking, bobblingly, though very ceremoniously, pee. The object was to see who could create the longest, dark streak along the tar surface of North Hiawatha. Fortunately, the world was a quieter place then, for over many such contests over a period of adolescent years, not once do I recall our parade ever being interrupted by oncoming head-lights. There were only the stars sprinkled above and the pee-ers below, three or four abreast, clumsily waddling down Hiawatha. I tell you, life was good. And that was about as outrageous as it ever got for us in the peace of the Garden.

On the banks their clubs they buried,
Buried all their warlike weapons.
Gitche Manito, the mighty,
The Great Spirit, the creator,
Smiled upon his helpless children.

Chapter Five and One-Third

....

Fire Aftermath

Following the fire that took the lives of the young mother and her baby, a delegation from the North End went to see the mayor to protest that the fire hydrants did not operate north of the tracks. City crews periodically flushed the water system in other parts of the city to keep it operating, but such never happened on our end of town. What could be done about it?

I have no idea what the mayor said in that meeting, but what was heard was, "Anyone stupid enough to live on the North End deserved what they got." Those words bounced around the neighborhood, reverberating in every home, shaking loose both anger and pain.

That fall when the mayor ran for re-election, every eligible voter from north of the tracks stepped into the voting booth, and the mayor was soundly defeated in his reelection bid. The mayor was unpopular, and the voter turnout was extraordinarily heavy, and he would have lost the election anyway, but the Northenders assumed full responsibility for the outcome, and felt a sense of involvement and pride not exactly common among them. One might say it was their finest hour.

Chapter Five and Two-Thirds

....

Home Coming

Ηow many times over the years did it happen? Twenty? Certainly no more than that. Always the same, it became familiar, yet never explained itself; I never learned its name.

It always happened without warning. While driving through a sleepy farming community, or walking down a previously unexplored street, I would see it. A building with big windows spanning the front, a singular door in the middle. The type of building that use to house a feed and seed store with its disarrangement of chicken waterers, incubators, and stacks of sacked grain. The kind of building that in pre-World War II days held an auto dealership, with the latest, shiny product of Detroit drawing kids to press their noses to the glass. Actually, the inside of the building was immaterial; the mystery belonged to the exterior. I would see it and suddenly be somewhere else, not in visual, but emotional, memory. Always it was a feeling experience. The time was freer, the world safer, the air cleaner, the sun brighter. Each time I would remain in the here and now, AND experience myself in that other captivating place, only I never knew where that other place was, except that it was like going home.

During the summer of 1982 I attended an Archives and History Conference in Louisville, Kentucky. On the return trip I followed the Ohio River westward as far as Hawesville, Kentucky, a river front town and the childhood home of my dad. I located the courthouse, intending to search for his birth record, but the hollow halls offered nothing but locked doors.

A young woman in the police station next door told me the courthouse closed on Thursday afternoons, and it was Thursday afternoon.

Not wanting the side-trip to be a total loss I decided to take a walking tour of the city, picturing how it may have looked when dad knew its streets seventy years before. The town, like the courthouse, was all but closed down; few people were about. Maybe because it was Thursday afternoon.

I stopped at the drug store to ask whether anyone remembered our family name. No one did. The same was true at a corner gas station. I did learn that the courthouse had burned down years before and that all records had been lost. If any evidence of my dad's passing through Hawesville existed, it would not be found on Main Street.

On a whim I headed for the river. I never had stood on the bank of the Ohio before, and this might be my only chance. Then I saw it. My building. The building of all those other buildings. A fading, white-frame structure with thin, aging pillars that held up the roof that extended out over the sidewalk. And an unusually high, cement step running the full width of the building. And the large glass panes. Evidently the local Republican organization used the building, as large, GOP posters hung in several of the windows.

Suddenly it was 1939. I was almost five years old. Our family had driven to Kentucky in our new-to-us Hudson Terraplane to visit my grandfather and other relatives. I first viewed this building from across the street, from the front yard of a family we were visiting. I asked permission to cross the street to see the building, but was told no. Nonetheless, once the adults went inside to visit, my sister Doris and I sneaked across to examine the building anyway.

I had to climb the front step because it was so high. The bottom portion of the windows were blacked out with some kind of material and I had to pull myself up to peek inside. What I saw was nondescript office space: a leather chair with brass tacks running around the back, a highback desk with compartments for this and that, and over that a large calendar, the kind that grain elevators and banks typically passed out at Christmas. And dust. Everything was dusty. That's all.

I have no inkling why that particular building made such a lasting impression on me; a very comfortable "feeling in my bones" that periodically presented itself. I do regret not knowing that those feelings were most probably replaying those of a four-year-old, and thus were a precious gift of innocence and wide-eyed wonder extended over time, feelings I cannot generate or recover by intent or effort. I'm glad I found the building, though I paid a heavy price for it. I have not had that *deja vu*-like experience again.

I share this story only because it's rooted in that year when we lived in the Johnson House, that period of time when the world began unfolding its wonders to me. I have learned to look upon children of that age with great fascination, knowing that wonderful things are coming together for them as they never may do so again. I'm very careful to offer them only the best of my own gifts. They may have lasting value.

Chapter Six

Chickens and Stuff

Many years ago I read that the owl, so often elevated as the symbol of wisdom, has the mental capacity of an earthworm. And I say, who has seriously measured the IQ of those humble, subterranean creatures? What tool was created to do so? Can we establish that some worms are more intelligent than others? Or are earthworms measured on scales made for chimpanzees or dogs, and so come up wanting? Or was the statement simply someone's way of discounting the fancied intelligence of the owl, and the earthworm seemed a likely comparison to which people would carry a concept?

Every time I hear someone disparage the "ignorant" creatures around us I suspect they are measuring with human yardsticks, and that this rather snobbish approach gives them permission to discount whatever creature they choose, and consequently, to do with said creature whatever they please. Still, one must take note that an earthworm has the tools to do quite nicely as a worm. The same can be said of owls. I, for instance, lack the gifts to fill either niche.

In 1940 the Gist family moved to their very own home on Second Avenue, just south and across the street from the McCurdy House. When we moved we took our "dumb" chickens with us. I grew up with these entertaining creatures, and they played a not insignificant role in my early years. For instance, the day I brought home my fellow kindergartener and very first friend, Donnie Borsma, I introduced him to the fun of herding chickens into the corner of the fenced-in chicken yard, and then catching them by the legs. This was in the Johnson house. We were small and barely a match for a flapping, struggling hen, and we both took repeated swats in the face in the attempt to capture one. Still, it was the very best thing I had to share with my guest.

When my folks raised chickens it was both for the eggs and the occasional chicken dinner. The chickens came under that awful, general term, "live stock," *i.e.*, living beings that we claimed to own. No one ever suggested the impropriety of that , and we went right on owning them, with all the assumed rights of proprietorship, including the dispensing of death, which happened repeatedly over the years.

Many people never have witnessed the "dance of death" performed by a beheaded chicken. Once decapitated, the poor, incomplete creature jumps frantically around, wings flapping and blood spewing everywhere. You have the option of holding their quivering bodies and draining the blood away, of course, but it is quicker to have two of three of them leaping about into eventual stillness before plunging them into the scalding hot water to make plucking easier.

Or one can do it the businesslike way my mother did when working at the Armour plant. There the poor, frightened, squawking creatures were hooked by the legs on a slowly moving conveyor that carried them first to the one who cut their throats, then to those who dunked and then dressed them, then finally, to one who singed the pin feathers from them. Mom, like the others, wore rubber aprons and knee-high boots to keep the blood from their clothes. Exterminations to human appetite come in many forms.

My older brother Kenny could never eat chicken. When he was three he watched as mother took chickens in hand, wrung their necks, dipped them into hot water, and gutted them. The horror of it connected to the smell of it, and both got wired somewhere inside him. To his dying day whenever a piece of chicken was placed before him, the smells of that earlier experience would uncomfortably wash over him. What he experienced was the uncomfortable reality that goes with eating flesh. Something must die, and usually in unpleasant ways.

Some people use an axe and a chopping block when killing a chicken for the evening meal, but the customary way in our yard was to take the chicken by the head and twirl the body, literally cranking the body from the head. This cruel and grotesque form of killing led naturally to the flopping, hopping, headless chicken spraying the grass with red. It's awesome how some among us simply continue to do things the way they always have been done, no matter how repellent the act. The last time I "cranked chickens" I was in my thirties. A member of our church congregation was selling spring fryers, and we bought twenty of them, drug them to the party, and dressed them. The whole process got to me that summer afternoon, and standing in the shade of a huge elm tree I suddenly realized that that was not who and what I wanted to be. For a while I ate chicken if someone else did the dirty work, but after a time I realized I didn't like that about me either, and finally, when the moment seemed right, I gave up eating chicken and other formerly living things altogether. I find that alive they fill a spiritual space much more satisfyingly than they fill a physical emptiness, dead.

I sometimes think of that New Testament passage where Jesus said not a sparrow falls to the ground without God taking notice. It's always been a favorite of mine, describing a God I can relate to. I remember one winter stepping to our front picture window and of seeing a dead sparrow beneath our bird feeder. I said to myself, "God's attention was focused right here in front of our window." I said it, but I didn't believe it. No form of consciousness was capable of being aware of every single thing that happens in the universe. Over the years, however, I've come to understand the verse. God knows when the sparrow falls to the ground because God is One with the sparrow . . . with the sparrow and all else, including the defenseless chicken in my hand about to be brutally dispatched. On reflection, a sobering thought.

Baby chickens were among the creatures we sometimes placed under a light bulb in a box in the basement. They needed the warmth. One year we actually hatched out a clutch of brown eggs with nothing more than the heat provided by that bulb. Edison had no idea how marvelous his invention was.

Every child should watch chickens hatch. They struggle greatly to get free from the shell, and children are eager to lend a helping hand, but must not; the striving is important to the process, and the chicks usually make it on their own, and will usually die if you help them. The miracle of hatching eggs is the yippee of the fowl world. What's even more fascinating is that an old cluck might spend two weeks laying a dozen eggs in a nest, and yet when it comes time for them to hatch they happen all in a bunch—within hours of each other.

For a few years we continued to gather eggs and eat chickens at the Gist Place. My parents allowed for the natural progression of the flock with an occasional cluck hen setting in the nest, which typically was an orange crate turned on its side, nailed to the coop wall, and lined with straw. Rats were a problem, and they would sneak in at night and steal baby chicks right from under the setting hen. Still, the clucks innocently managed to bring small families into this people-and-rat-eat-chicken world.

After a while the chicken wire came down and the coop became a storage shed. Still, I continued raising chickens on my own, and they were free to roam the yard. Each spring the hatchery would go through all the peeping hatchlings, separating the males from the females. It was no fun being born male because typically you didn't survive. The money was in the producers, the hens. So one could go to the hatchery and get a couple dozen, baby, roosters-to-be for nothing, and for several years I did. Although I did not think of it at the time, this was a temporary rescue of life from certain death. It never occurred to me to ask how the hundreds of little male peepers were disposed of, but I suspect it was not a pretty sight. Neither did I ever find out how one distinguished a male from a female chick, but the hatchery people obviously knew what they were doing. Only once did we get a hen by mistake.

Chickens are notoriously easy to train and I would always have a flock that came running from every direction when I whistled. I sometimes did it just to show other people that they would come, but of course they came with high expectations of being fed, for that's how I trained them. Each time feed was put in the trough or scattered on the ground I simply whistled, and within a few days the pattern was learned.

Chickens, like all birds, have remarkable eyesight, and are quicker than humans, at least when spotting and gobbling up worms from freshly turned soil. Before it was removed, the best place to find big, fat angle worms and nightcrawlers, and the easiest place to dig, was in the chicken yard, only you had to expose a hundred worms to get a dozen. The slightest movement of worm, indeed, the slightest flash of worm flesh, was enough for a chicken, and it typically would have the worm before I saw it. And just as they later learned to hustle to me when I whistled, so the penned flock quickly gathered when I walked inside the fence with potato fork and tin can in hand. When one happened, the other automatically followed. Simple stimulus–response.

I have found this Pavlovian connection useful in my own life. For instance, each morning for years I dissolved some Questran Light (a cholesterol lowering medication) in apple juice, and drank it. I didn't like the stuff, and so formed the habit of reading jokes or remembering humorous events to generate some good, health-giving laughter as I took it. Like a chicken, it did not take the body long to make the connection, and in time, laughter or no laughter, the stuff went down more easily. I even fantasized that the health-giving benefits of laughter were now triggered by the gritty sensation of the Questran. Who knows?

Anyway, I'm a simple sort, and that is something I picked up from dumb chickens.

Chapter Seven

Goodbye Gulliver, it was Good to Know You

Today is October 3, 1997. This morning I took Sammy, our dachshund, for a walk in Riverside Park. Sammy suffers from congestive heart failure and soon will be gone. I watched as leaves floated down from the trees, many settling onto the surface of the Rum River to be gently carried away. Trees understand the times, letting go of what cannot be held, trusting in eventual renewal. I watched, even listened, and reluctantly tried to accept. But I have not yet fully learned the wisdom of the trees.

Still, a part of me recognizes that growth largely comes from letting go, that and unlearning. A small child lets go of the Easter Bunny, but hangs onto Santa Claus a while longer. Adults seriously walking the spiritual path lay to rest one god after another, shedding their tears at each burial, then awaiting, or going in search of, a greater god.

Children let go of many things as they create and recreate the world, and of course, culture systematically imprints them with outrageous bits and pieces that they are "supposed to believe." On the other hand, children often see through our adult stuff and force us to see what we miss of our world. It's truly a lovely process to observe.

For instance, in the early seventies Norma and I attended the movie *Snow White*. In a late scene the witch has created the poison apple and sets out to offer it to Snow White. She descends the long, winding, stone, staircase that leads to the bowels of the castle. Spider webs drape every corner, rats scurry about, and the witch's eyes are full of fury and self-satisfaction. I don't recall but she may have been cackling fiendishly, for she is about to eliminate her beautiful rival. She carries the poisoned apple in a basket. As this scene unfolds, a little girl sitting directly behind us, a girl probably four years of age, says quite loudly and distinctly to her mother, "My, but she has a lovely wicker basket." My wicker basket story happened when I was four. At the movies at the Government Indian School where I saw the animated movie: *Gulliver's Travels.* I fell in love with the gentle giant, and almost as completely, with his shirt. Never before had I seen such a wonderful one. It was slit down the front about a third of its length, and each side of the slit sported buttons. Small narrow bands of cloth spanned the space of the slit, button to button. It was as beautiful as Gulliver was magnificent. The next day I searched through the *Montgomery Ward* catalog for such a shirt. None were shown. My brother and sisters hardly knew what I was talking about; the shirt had not registered in their memories.

Disappointed though I was, I maintained a passionate admiration for Gulliver, so when shortly after seeing the movie mom told me that the biggest man in the whole, wide world was coming to Pipestone, I was euphoric.

Oh, the anticipation. The giant was coming. The giant was coming. But what a wait. In reality it was but a few days, but I remember it as interminable as I entertained myself with visions of the giant towering over the buildings and trees of our town. As he moved among us he would so carefully place his feet where no harm could be done, for giants are gentle creatures. I also nurtured the hope that of all the townspeople, he would choose me to hold in his palm to talk to.

On the morning of the day of his visit, I went outside to scan the skyline in hopes of catching that first glimpse of him. Nothing. In time, Betty, Shirley and I hurried up town to where a large crowd had gathered around a flatbed parked on Hiawatha Avenue between the Calumet Hotel and Herold's Shoe Store. But where was the giant? What was going on? Slowly it dawned on me that giants lived only in fairy tales. Obviously this giant was not as big as Gulliver. We worked our way around the crowd until finally we had a partial view of several men on the bed of the truck. Betty pointed and said, "There he is. Do you see him?" I did not.

"There, right there," she said, pointing. "Now do you see him?"

I didn't, but said I did. And that was the end of the matter. Just like that my expectations dissipated. Gulliver-size giants were make-believe, and if I could not pick out of a crowd the biggest man in the world, then the so-called giants of the real world were not all that fantastic. I resolutely concluded that on, July 28th, 1939, at the age of four-years-eight-months. Still, friends have told me I didn't quit believing, I just transferred my fascination and comfort with giants unto God. Perhaps.

The connection between size and power and kind gentleness pops up periodically in my memory, and is illustrated by a story my dad told me. He spent his early years in Kentucky where his dad worked as a farm hand. I never knew my grandfather as a person. Only on one occasion did I spend time with him. On a rare visit to our home he, dad, and I went fishing at Lake Shetek. We fished from the Vallhala Island dike. What I remember about granddad that day was that he scolded me for taking my line in and casting it our so often. "You won't catch any fish that way," he said. I noticed he was not catching any his way either.

This winter I met for the first time a retired minister by the name of Rodney Gist. I had heard about him for years and was pleased for the opportunity to spend a couple hours with him. As far as we can determine we are not related, at least within the last four generations, but curiously, he knew my grandfather. He told me of working with him as a seventeen-year-old during threshing season. My grandfather was eighty-five years old at the time, but worked all day stacking sheaves. As Rodney said of him, "Work was his life." My own father was similarly blessed with health. He played on the church's soft ball team well into his sixties, and at 86 he bought himself a new fishing boat, and also a large snow blower so he could clean sidewalks for the neighborhood elderly.

The "giant" story I'm sneaking up on comes through my dad from his dad. Grandpa was among a group of field hands who toiled together day after day under the hot Kentucky sun. One of my grandfather's cowork-ers was a big Black man named *Mose*. Along about mid-afternoon when everyone was wearing out, this huge bundle of manhood would say to my grandfather, "You just slow down and take it easy now; let ol Mose carry the load the rest of the way." And according to dad, this giant would double his efforts at scything grain. Appropriately, a vital part of my religious faith is that power is never to be used "over," but always "under;" that power is a mandate to protect and help those who are weaker. I consistently debate with hunters and trappers who argue that their activities are God-ordained because God gave us "dominion," and my reply is that power, dominion, always is to be used as did our *domini*, in creative, undergirding ways. They don't always get the connection between the words.

From the crowd that day on Hiawatha avenue the three of us moved to Herold's where the giant's shoes were on display. The store had spon-sored his visit and so had the privilege of showing off his footwear. I have to admit, I was impressed with those shoes, and we all agreed that a baby could be bedded down in one of them.

Here's the delicious part. The story of the giant was not completed until I reached the age of sixty-one-years-four-months. In the archives. The probable reason for my failure to catch a once-in-a-life-time glimpse of the 8' 8 3/4" Robert Wadlo is that the poor man spent most of his time sitting down, because standing was so difficult for him. I must have caught him sitting. He wasn't quite as large as the legendary King Og in the Bible, whose casket (or bedstead) allegedly measured Thirteen-and-a-half feet by five-feet, but before he left town Wadlo reached up and left a pencil mark on the light pole outside the hotel. It later was measured at eleven feet. The man was no Gulliver, but was, indeed, a giant.

Chapter Seven
and a Half

Other Somebodies

Was Robert Wadlo getting rich or just trying to survive? I don't know, but clearly the price he paid to visit us, and other towns across America, was enormous. That year he traveled tens of thousands of miles sitting in the back of a seven-passenger, 1937 Plymouth. The front seat was removed to give him leg room, mostly straight out in front, because the back seat was necessarily lowered almost to the floor to accommodate his height. This eliminated most of the cushioning. The year before his stop in Pipestone he traveled 37,000 miles in the Plymouth, and 1939s' schedule was as heavy.

Not all roads led to Pipestone, of course, but three railroad lines and two intersecting highways kept its doors open to the grander world beyond. Wadlo found us, and so did a variety of notables of the second and third rank. They popped in often enough to lend a cosmopolitan air to our burgeoning community. For instance, during the war Smiley Burnette (Frog Milhouse), Gene Autry's movie sidekick, entertained us one night at the Orpheum. I still remember someone getting up and walking up the aisle during his performance, and Burnette saying, "Please don't leave, the show's not over yet." Then as the man continued on, "Well, if you gotta go, you gotta go." Such *savoir-faire*. The house roared in polished appreciation.

Only months after Wadlo's appearance, another celebrated luminary chose my fifth birthday to visit us. Aunt Jemima. Right off the pancake mix package and into our town. She spent the day at Steinberg's grocery store. We, of course, had to go see her and have some free pancakes. What a wonderful world I had been born into.

Chapter Eight

Thank You Miss Higgins

I don't remember what Miss Higgins, my first-grade instructor, looked like. But she was a Miss Higgins. *Miss Marjorie Higgins.* In those days the gods influenced the naming of teachers, and we first-graders spoke her's with admiration and respect. Miss Higgins. She could not have pursued any other profession. Her destiny locked in the day her mom and dad named her Marjorie.

The same thing happened to my second grade teacher, *Miss Olive Von Sien.* I know what she looked like because some photographer took a group picture of we rambunctious tatterdemalions, standing, quite naturally, in front of the school, and Miss Von Sien is in it. She actually wore very thick glasses befitting such a confidence-inspiring name.

Maybe if you put a "Miss" in front of any name it will sound like a school marm, but what about, *Ernestine Sanden*? Miss Sanden controlled our fourth grade class with the moxy befitting her sturdy name. One of her fellow teachers was *Olga Skailand.* Can you not picture and trust this dispenser of knowledge?

Parents in those days truly understood the significance of naming. One of the clearest examples of that unfolded when Mr. and Mrs. Wakefield envisioned their infant daughter growing up to teach junior high social studies, and so gave her the name "Daisy." *Miss Daisy Wakefield.* Do you hear its pedagogical ring? The diminutive Miss Daisy always kept a dainty, lace-edged hankie tucked in her left hand. She also snapped the fingers of that hand at we students to command our attention, but unfortunately the hankie, as often as not, muffled the authority of her well-intentioned snap. Actually, her name determined that all rough edges be softened.

So, too, can you not imagine being thirteen and having to report to the principal's office of Miss *Gladys Evans*? The substantial, grey-haired Miss Gladys Evans? The decent, fair, but tough Miss Gladys Evans? Miss Gladys Evans who handed out detention time for classroom infractions and tardiness?

I learned geography from this gifted teacher, and also received instruction about life. My steady habit of arriving late to school required frequent trudges to her desk for a "late pass," and the assignment of detention time (I did most of my school work in the detention hall). One morning I stood behind a girl from the grade ahead of me who offered a really fine excuse for her tardiness. She told Miss Evans that she wasn't going to come to school that morning because she was not feeling well, but then at the last minute felt better and decided she'd better come anyway. Miss Evans kindly inquired after her health, then issued a pass, but assigned no detention time. Wow! I hadn't known such a combination was possible. I saved that girl's marvelous excuse for an entire year, from the 7th to the 8th grade, carefully delivering it one cold morning with a slight cough and a spirit of contrition--I truly was sorry to be showing up late, but not feeling well I wasn't going to come at all. The remarkable Miss Gladys complimented me for my good memory--she remembered the previous moment as clearly as I did--explaining that such a fine excuse was not in keeping with my unsurpassed record of indefensible tardiness, and that in spite of my out-of-character attempt, she would, nonetheless, issue detention time. She did it with the sensitivity of someone breaking off a relationship, and I left her office feeling I had been treated fairly. Such finesse was predestined because of her name, you see.

In Pipestone High the most fitting name of all--better than *Mr. James Figgie*, *Mr. Noah Nelson*, and *Miss Byrma Jones*, was certainly Miss Vorce. *Miss Alta Vorce*. Every school system in the country has its Miss Vorce. A disciplinarian's disciplinarian, as set in her ways as a rusty nail in a fence post. She had been in the school system forever. She taught English, and we learned it. At least I did. She also taught Latin. "Alta Vorce." The uninitiated might quite fittingly mistake her name for a Latin declension, but no, it stood for "teacher," and that she was. Her time and place in history had taught her hard-edged discipline, and some of it had settled in her face. Even her smile seemed stern. I could not imagine her outside the classroom, and sometimes wondered what she did when she was not in the school building. Most students complained about her, many did not like her, but I was not among them. I feared her, but also enjoyed her, believing she had our best interests at heart.

On the morning of "Graduation Night" I received an urgent telephone call from the senior high principal, Mr. Swenson. He informed me that

Miss Vorce had pulled my name from the list of those eligible to graduate. It seems my final, ten-page term paper was missing a page, and she would not let me graduate with an "incomplete." With something akin to awe in his voice Mr. Swenson assured me she would do exactly what she said (Everyone's boat was in danger of being swamped by the redoubtable Miss Vorce--even a principal's). I immediately scrounged through the pile of notebooks and papers in the corner of my bedroom and with great relief found the missing page. I jumped on my bike and headed for school, wondering what would happen if I could not find Miss Vorce.

It was early June. The birds were singing, the sun shone brightly, indeed, the world stepped lightly, and why not, school was over. By contrast, the interior of Pipestone High was a sepulcher with stairs, its resting halls resentful of the click, click, click of my hurried step. Up two flights of stairs to the unlighted, third floor, past locked, glass-paneled doors, I made my way to Miss Vorce's classroom. The door was ajar and she was at her post . Blinded by the belligerence of youth, I did not understand that she was there, not because she had work to do, not because she would not rather have been elsewhere, not even, I think, as the captive of her christening day, but only to be available to a careless seventeen-year-old so he could turn in page seven and move on with his life. I did not say thank you. I was in no mood to say it. I didn't like her at that moment. Now, it's probably too late, but I wish to say it anyway. Thank you Miss Vorce.

So, my experiences in public school ended with Miss Vorce, even as they began with Miss Higgins. Though I can not see Miss Higgin's face, I can see her hand at that moment on that very first day of school when she went to the board, drew a vertical line, then a second one, and finally bridged the two together with a horizontal one, and said, "This is an "H." Wow! We were on our way to reading, to learning, and I was enthralled with a fascination that has never left me.

H was the first letter in HERE, and HERE was the first word in HERE WE GO, UP, UP, UP. Dick and Jane were climbing the ladder on a slide and of course in time would go DOWN, DOWN, DOWN. I tired of those plotless books long before we quit using them, but that first morning, September 3, 1940, was a glorious beginning. Her hand tracing out that first letter so neatly on the lined black board, neatly as only a school teacher could, resides so clearly in my head that I could go to the seat I sat in that morning, the angle of my view is so precise in my mind.

We were beginning. We were going, up, up, up.

Thank you, too, Miss Higgins.

Chapter Eight and a Half

Teresa Ross

"Here we go, up, up, up. Here we go, down, down, down." That was Dick and Jane. That also was Dick in pursuit of Teresa.

Miss Higgins may have provided the brilliant daylight of knowledge from the front of the classroom, but the sanctifying glow of each new day shone warmly from a seat next to the windows. There sat Charlie Brown's little "red-haired girl," an angel without feathers. Actually, her hair was not red but the color or rain-washed straw, and it fell around her shoulders, framing a face as pretty as any that ever graced a wall calendar. Her name was Teresa Ross.

I learned by pieces that this goddess-in-the-making lived . . . north of the tracks . . . in the second house . . . along the tar road . . . with her grandmother.

Like good ol Charlie, I desperately wanted to meet her, but was too uncertain to initiate anything. I devised a foolproof plan. I would roll a car tire up and down, back and forth, in front of her grandma's place. Eventually she would surely look out the window or come out into the yard and see me, and admire how good a tire roller I was. Surely her admiration would lead her to come forth from behind the picket fence and speak to me.

Up and down, up and down Hiawatha I rolled that tire. I rolled it every day for a week, trying not to look obvious. The house was small and certainly had little room inside in which a girl could entertain herself. And it had windows that faced the road. But not once did my Teresa make an appearance. Not once did I see a curtain move as she secretly admired my tire rolling prowess.

After a time I gave up the effort, and before Christmas Teresa disappeared, from the classroom, from behind the dainty curtains, and from my life, perhaps to be reunited with her mother. I never knew. And Miss Higgins never explained the empty seat next to the windows.

Chapter Nine

....

When Butterflies Cry

"Universe" can be translated as "one song." The world is made up of notes and melodies and harmonies, and we get lost when we live discordant lives.

Some say God lives in silence. Maybe so. There is much to be said for silence. I have a cat, Hash, that lives thusly, virtually never meowing. He snores, but that doesn't count. Our Dachshund Sammy barks only to challenge intruders, otherwise he too lives in quietude. At times I join the secret wisdom of both creatures to get the feel of living between the notes and on the rests. It's a legitimate place to pause, for those spaces are essential to the music.

I trust that God is good at harmony. I know we are the experts in discord and cacophony. Earlier I asked, "What is the sound of conception?" It was a serious question. Everything in existence has a vibration. All atoms, every molecule, each cell, dances. I see this when I look at auras, whether that of a road sign or that of the woman pushing the shopping cart up the aisle ahead of me. We are fields of energy. Our bodies are a grand ballroom, and when we are healthy, the orchestra is marvelously tuned and each element sweepingly in step. The world's a ballroom too. Even in conception, the waiting egg and the swarming sperm contribute to life's symphony. Scientists tell us that the electron shell of the carbon atom, that atom so essential to life, follows the laws of harmonics, producing the tone scale, C-D-E-F-G-A, which is also the hexachord of Gregorian chant. Music and life, life and music, are intricately entwined. Each being is a musical event.

Many years ago I watched a documentary, which included an episode of a young, cow elephant in labor. She was birthing her first calf, and was frightened and tense. The process was not going at all well, and both the unborn calf's and the cow's lives were endangered. A park ranger and a medicine man approached the distraught creature and attached some device that allowed them to monitor her heartbeat. They then retreated a discrete distance and had a drummer beat out the heart rhythm on a log drum, the rhythm of the cow's life. This sympathetic drumming greatly calmed her, she relaxed, and shortly gave birth to a healthy calf. So it is for us all. When we are in tune, in sync with the rhythms of Creation, things proceed as they were intended.

A skilled counselor picks up the breathing pattern of the client, matching it breath for breath, and by so doing, establishes an unconscious sense of connectedness and trust, which facilitates the counseling process. When even two lives begin building harmony, healing can follow.

Like the drummer, like the psychologist, we consciously can live with a sympathetic beat, but because we are quite skilled at discord, we have to work at it.

Three things life has taught me. First, that budding, Roman Catholic, female, writers must write about their experiences in Catholic school, and particularly about the nuns, before they move on to other things.

Second, males, some man's son all, if ever they put pen to paper, are driven to explore the father-son relationship. It tugs and draws at them like nothing else in life.

The third truth is that all male vegetarians clearly remember the first sparrow they shot with the BB gun they got for their tenth birthday (I bet you didn't know any of these, right?).

I'm among those who vividly remembers the latter. I was at the Dredgeditch bridge. A sparrow sat high up in the willows that grew on the bank at the base of that concrete structure, no better able to contain its song than the flowers were able to imprison their fragrances. Unfortunately, it sat at eye level with me. I raised my shiny, new Red Ryder carbine, pulled the trigger, and without a sound or flutter the little creature simply dropped from its perch, bouncing and caroming through the branches to the mud below. That bird survived the harsh Minnesota winter only to have its song senselessly stilled in the gentle sunlight of a spring morning. By me.

I enjoy and therefore miss the chirping of an absent sparrow, but what of the music and discord too fine for my ears? When I was eight I decided to make a butterfly collection, and spent a bright, July morning catching a variety of these flitting flowers, placing them in a large jar with the obligatory holes punched in the lid. Once satisfied that I had a good start toward a collection, I determined to kill them. But how to do it? I solved the problem by clamping their two wings together between my fingers, and repeatedly piercing the butterfly's body with a hatpin. But they wouldn't die. One after another failed to go still under my ruthless attack.

Now if pain operates at the cellular level, and I'm convinced it does— even amoebae retreat before pain and will thicken the cell wall in an attempt to armor themselves against it—then those small creatures suffered horribly at my hands. Some would call that an evil act.

During *Adolph Eichman's* trial in Palestine for war crimes, a man came out of the courtroom one day distraught and weeping. His sobbed, "But he's only a man, he's only a man." He struggled to comprehend how so much terror and death could come from an ordinary, human being. Evil wears a human face, and can masquerade even in innocence. I was eight years old, and learning to stop my ears to the music.

We need to "listen." To the music in the flight of a bird, to the harmony in a school of fish, the crescendo in billowing clouds. And when we begin hearing the tinkle of dripping dewdrops, we may, at last, pick up the trembling vibrations from within a pin-pierced butterfly.

A butterfly has all the appearance of being carefully constructed, and if God gave so much attention and detail to it, what must an angel be like? And I reply, perhaps the angels have not been so grandly designed, only differently. In a Creation each thing, each being, is a sacred and unique instance of the indivisible Whole. In their created individuality, they share common ground. The glory of a butterfly may be very much different from the glory of an angel, but it is the same glory shared. How else is one to understand Creation's "One Song?"

To believe in a loving Creator God places all beings equidistant from the heart and hand of the Creator, and from each other. Creation is Oneness and a continuously unfolding act of love in which we are privileged to participate. That summer morning I acted as though I was above and outside the Oneness. I would never have said it that way, but at that moment I experienced my separation from something important, only I wasn't sure what. Life can only be lived in relationship, sympathetically or otherwise. My "otherwise" grievously disrupted the harmony that morning. I had not yet comprehended the indivisible Oneness of existence, had not yet learned that in this wondrous Creation, when butterflies cry, angels weep.

Chapter Ten

Spotty

In his old age he didn't have a tooth in his head. When the man from the lumber yard wanted to measure the house for the new windows dad had ordered, dad warned him, "The dog won't bother you if you simply walk around, but he won't let you touch the house. Understand?"

"No problem," the man assured him. "I deal with dogs all the time."

Sure enough, as he made his way around the outside at 716 2nd Ave. N.E., a longhaired, black and white spitz-airedale followed him, apparently friendly and curious. Reassured by the dog's neighborly demeanor the man decided to get a precise measurement and reached up and laid his tape measure to the window casement. Bam, bam, just like that he was gummed twice and warned thereafter by growls and curled lip. Unhurt, but dampened in enthusiasm, he withdrew until dad could be present.

From the inside of the house no dog was ever a more fierce protector of a home. The upper half of both the front and back doors of our place had large windows; people could see in, Spotty could see out. Any time anyone came to the door Spotty would repeatedly hurl himself against the door, barking, snarling, snapping, lips pulled back, doing everything in his power to get to the intruder on the other side of the door. When he had teeth he truly was frightening. No mindless people ever visited us, so everyone withdrew, uncertain that mere wood could long keep them separated from such a menace.

Spotty did not lose his teeth through old age or disease, but by ramming into passing cars. He owned Second Avenue and no moving vehicles were allowed to pass unchallenged. Now, most dogs didn't slide into the Fords, Hudsons, and DeSotos that they chased, a fast-spinning tire whacking them alongside the head. Spotty did, but the collision was both typical and non-deterring; and he had a legitimate excuse. He ran around on two legs, both on the right side of his body. Remarkably, he could run about as fast as any other dog, but he was short on brakes.

We never knew exactly what happened though we suspected that Spotty was crouched in the long grass in the ditch, waiting to challenge the oncoming Ford tractor. When he made his attack, he was not prepared for the rapidly slicing teeth of the city's mowing machine that was cutting the grass in the roadside ditches. His front leg was almost totally severed, the back haunch (is that the right word?), chewed to the bone. While the city employee fought to get the mower stopped, Spotty somehow scrambled out onto the boulevard.

I was not there, but one of my sisters fortunately was, and she called dad who immediately rushed home. He tenderly picked the dog up and carried him to the unused chicken coop in the back yard, laying him on a braided rug from the entry way. Then reluctantly he called the veterinarian to come out to put Spotty to sleep. Following the call he went to the front steps to await the vet, only to find the blood-spattered Spotty lying there. Amazed, he again carried him to the coop, hoping the dog would not exacerbate his pain by struggling out again, but when he left, Spotty followed, loping along on his two right-side legs.

Dad was prepared to put this dog to sleep, but when the vet came, rather than asking for the needle and syringe, he asked him to give the dog something for pain and infection and do his best at patching him up. The vet did, and almost miraculously, Spotty survived. No, that's not quite the right word for him. He triumphed.

For the rest of his life, and he lived a full one, he loped along on those two legs. In time the front one healed sufficiently so that he could stand on it, and as he galloped along it would lightly touch down and give additional support. As I rode my bike he followed me everywhere. Distance was never a problem, and as far as we could determine, he never developed arthritis. Indeed, no dog ever lived more fully.

I grew up believing that when strange dogs come together they fight because Spotty immediately hurled himself into snarling, snapping conflict with every unknown dog that came around. Little children could crawl all over him, and he and I would mock fight regularly in the living room, and from the sound and fury it sounded as though I was being torn and ripped, but never did I receive so much as a scratch. Zipper, our little Rat Terrier, would sleep on Spotty's full and fluffy tail. But when it came to strange dogs crossing the boundaries he maintained around our property, the fight was immediate and for real. He got along okay with the close neighborhood dogs, they were like a loosely knit pack, and he would follow me all over town and never start a fight, but dogs from outside our area were like a magnet for him; when he saw them he attacked them.

On reflection, I have learned much from this orneriest and most faithful of all dogs. For instance, after the accident, he never won a fight, AND he never was beaten. When in battle dogs often mount up on their hind legs together, and when this happened, Spotty with his single rear leg, would be knocked over and the other dog would have the advantage. Still, he always was the aggressor and he never quit. Never. We tried to break him of fighting, for his own sake and that of other dogs, but totally without success. We could only try to keep him relatively restrained and away from the canine crowd. He spent many summer afternoons on a leash on the clothesline to keep him close by.

Up the street from us lived an older kid, Bud, who moved in a different circle from those at the lower end of the neighborhood. He was older, bigger, and tougher than the rest of us. In later years his idea of fun was to go driving on a Saturday afternoon, shooting all the farm cats he ran across. I once released a cat from one of his leghold traps along the Dredge and he got all upset. He would have killed the cat.

He delighted in siccing (is that a word?) his dog unto Spotty, and because they were of similar size, it was a fair dogfight. But then he began encouraging both his and his neighbor's black lab to the attack. They would catch Spotty and me coming home from town or school, and the fight usually took place in the deep wide ditch along Hiawatha. With two on one Spotty always took a beating, but every time the other dogs retreated Spotty renewed the attack. Always I was afraid for him. The much larger dog was almost twice his size, and he would take Spotty by the throat and shake him, dragging him through the long grass of the ditch. When at last Spotty fought free he would hurl himself right back and as likely as not wind up being shaken by the throat again. I figure only his longhaired coat prevented him from being ripped open.

I heard an animal psychologist once say that if a dog gets his way one time out of twenty-five he thinks he's winning. Maybe it was that kind of canine mentality at work here, Spotty never seemed to recognize that he was getting the worst of it, and yet because the other dogs often tried backing away, he must have thought he was winning. They fought because they were incited to, Spotty fought because it was his nature. He had too much heart for his own good.

If I had possessed Spotty's courage I would have challenged this bigger kid and taken a beating. Instead, I would struggle to grab Spotty in those fleeting seconds when the dogs were separated, and eventually would manage to pull him away. This always was scary for me because the first year we had this remarkable dog it got into a fight with Hallanhan's black dog at the Armour Plant (I was bitten four times in my youth, each time by a black dog), and as I tried to break it up I was severely bitten. Fifty-five years later I still have the faint scars on my upper arm.

The world was different then. Being bitten by a dog, at least on the north end of town, was no big deal. If you delivered newspapers, you were likely to get bit. Twice Spotty bit people, both times, people on bikes. Each was reported to the police and each time we had to do something with Spotty, but it never occurred to anyone to sue, as would likely happen today.

For a while Spotty loped around with a strap bound around his long snout. When dad realized he had trouble drinking, he devised a wire affair, not unlike the wire screen around a trouble light, through which he could drink. It was unpadded and must have been uncomfortable, though it never seemed to bother him, and in time it was removed.

Anyway, Bud was scary, at least to me. I once watched as he repeatedly kicked with his heavily booted foot another kid from the neighborhood that he had bested in a fight. This boy was two years older than me, bigger, and considered a ruffian in his own right. In this instance he could do nothing to help himself, but simply curled up and accepted the stomping. Like most of us in such a situation, his will came to the fore and he refused to get up and go home as Bud was trying to get him to do. He was no physical match for Bud in a fight. He was beaten. And because a crowd was watching, he probably felt shamed, but he would have died before he yielded himself to the satisfaction of his tormentor; he was not going to be owned. I think most creatures are that way. And most of us.

When we lived in Ohio we had a fenced-in yard, and one evening a neighbor's beagle came over as I was closing the gates for the night. I tried to shoo him out of the yard, but for whatever reason, this dog decided he wasn't going to leave. I called him, yelled at him, tried pushing him, to which he would snap and snarl. Afraid I would be bitten, I began prodding him at a distance with a stick--more snarling. He had his feet planted and he was not going to be moved. It became a contest of wills. I moved to the other side of the fence and reached over and whacked him with the stick. More snarls. I picked up a hoe handle, more substantial than the stick, and whacked him again. Finally I came to my senses and realized I was hurting him, and backed off and went into the house. When his doggie spirit at last moved him, he trotted on home. The next day when he came over, he wagged his tail when he saw me, and trotted over to make up, the episode from the night before obviously forgotten. We have so much to learn from God's creatures. How marvelously they are put together on the inside.

I once showed a film series in our church on the "family." The man featured was nationally known and considerably more conservative than me and the people of my congregation, but because some members requested it, I publicized and ran the series. It was well received by some. Not by me.

In one of the first two films the speaker detailed how he had had a confrontation with his dog, clearly a test of will as I just described, but as a human he was not going to let a lesser creature win such a contest. Human superiority had to be demonstrated, dominion had to be exercised (he obviously interpreted dominion to mean domination), and he set out to break the dogs will. Through thoroughly cruel and repeated beatings, that is what he at last did. The dog's will was broken, man was again victorious, and he saw himself as the champion of right and good or some such nonsense. At the point of his cruelty he lost me and my respect, and I regretted the booking to which I was committed. He also preached the necessity of parents winning in tests of wills with their children. His approach to life is not the approach I want taken in my family, or any one else's. I sometimes despair that he is so widely acclaimed by those who would tame and civilize their children. I especially hate it when cruelty is chartered by Scripture, and abhor the idea that breaking the will of any creature is something positive. For him it was.

Most people have a great deal of dogginess in them. They can plant their feet and say, "Do whatever you want, but you are not going to own me." Though I was afraid of taking a physical beating from Bud, my real fear was of being shamed, of getting beat in front of others, maybe with no recourse but to lay in the ditch and take a stomping. If I have any macho spirit in me, and that is questionable, it resides in that fear of being shamed.

One day coming home from school, Bud and two of his friends intercepted me and Spotty. Each of the three had their dogs, two of them at least twenty pounds heavier than Spotty. All three dogs were sicced onto him, and the battle was engaged. Poor Spotty, he jumped up, was knocked down, and dragged through the grass by the throat and shaken like a large, stuffed animal, with the other two darting in and out from different directions, nipping and biting. Each time he was released he threw himself back into the attack. In the world of dogs he and I were part of the same pack and pack members instinctively, passionately, join forces on one another's behalf. Poor Spotty, he was part of a two-member pack, and the part that was me supplied him with no support. He was entirely on his own. The fight went on longer than I thought he could survive, but he wouldn't back off, and the others were enjoying the fray. Bud especially, who for reasons I never quite understood, hated Spotty. He would have felt no remorse in seeing him killed. I felt angry that I didn't know what to do, frustrated that I didn't know how to be angry and aggressive, feeling like, acting like, a wimp. My dog needed me and I was not there for him.

Then, somewhere in the ditch I located a hefty stick and began beating the other dogs off. Each time I got them to retreat Spotty attacked them again. I suspect that if Bud could have found a stick he would have taken me on, or maybe, maybe he realized at long last what was going on. Maybe he didn't want his dog getting knocked senseless. I never knew. But the others at long last pulled their dogs off and I managed to get my arms around Spotty's neck and dragged him out of fighting distance.

I was in tears most of the way home. I had been frightened for my companion. I was enraged at my lack of effectiveness when anger and aggressiveness were called for. I slumped down on the grass with Spotty, who remarkably seemed none the worse for wear, though those dog bites had to have bruised him severely. With tears running down my cheeks I told him I was sorry, sorry that I was such a poor friend. Sorry I was of so little help. I joined the ranks of the disciples who failed Jesus.

Spotty? He simply moved closer and began licking the tears from my face. The child who first suggested that God was so proud of dogs that he gave them his name, only backwards, was right. And that afternoon I was the recipient of divine, doggy grace.

I pray that God has a place in heaven for such gallant and noble creatures.

Chapter Ten and a Half

....

Spotty Spin Off

The Biblical Job advises us to let the other creatures instruct us, but as a boy I was not smart enough to learn the valuable lessons that Spotty presented to me. Indeed, I learned rather late in life what wonderful spiritual advisors dogs can be. It's more than the obvious—that a dog is a good listener. Or loyal. Or courageous, as was Spotty. Even more it is that dogs take things as they are without conjuring up ways to make themselves unhappy. Small children possess this wisdom, we older children seldom do.

For instance, one recent year we were troubled by box elder bugs. Those silly, orange and black creatures that never seem to do anything but walk around, and under certain conditions, congregate with other box elder bugs. That summer people in the neighborhood were almost frantic in their consternation over these "invaders." They sprayed them from trees and garage walls with garden hoses, sought out effective pesticides, whatever. One afternoon I observed our dachshund Sammy watch a box-elder bug crossing the front steps right under his nose. A bit curious, he sniffed it, found nothing interesting, and certainly nothing disturbing, and got back to the serious business of enjoying a summer afternoon nap. I decided to follow suit and "included" the bug in my world. And the irritation I felt at its presence vanished immediately. It's important to know what is significant and what is not, especially when it comes to expending energy.

On the occasion of his 80th birthday the sculptor Henry Moore was asked the secret of life. His answer:

> The secret of life is to have a task, something you devote your entire life to, something you bring everything to, every minute of every day for your whole life.

And the most important thing is—it must be something you cannot possibly do.

Before I read the Moore quote I had already learned about singleness of mind from Spotty, and later from Sammy. Periodically, a pair of jackrabbits will explore our back yard in the early morning. Sammy's a dachshund. An overweight dachshund. An aging dachshund. One with an allergy, which keeps his feet perpetually sore and often swollen. But just let him at those jackrabbits. He gives them his very best effort, and doesn't quit the chase even after they've disappeared from sight. He simply shifts to his nose, obviously believing he still has a chance to catch one. Even in eventual failure he comes back, head and tail held high, in obvious good spirits, perhaps thinking about the next time.

To my knowledge he never has caught up with but one sizable creature, a woodchuck, and I rescued that from him (or he from it), with apologies. Both were well bloodied when I intervened, but Sammy obviously enjoyed the fight.

Apart from woodchucks, Sammy is shamelessly big on mice. He will spend mornings and afternoons sniffing out their trails through the grass, and when he is in pursuit of one—obvious from the rapidly fanning tail— he gives it his all. But they have a way of evading him. He gets an occasional mouse only because his almost constant companion, Hash, a black-and-white cat, catches them and turns them over to him. Still, Sammy is propelled through his days by anticipation and doggy-determination. And I watch his "Yes and Yippee!," smile, give thanks, and learn.

The only good photo I could find of Spotty

Chapter Eleven

....

Hell in a Kave

On a recent trip to my hometown I discovered that the intersection of highways 75 and 30 (when I was young, 75 and 47) now boasts a MacDonald's, complete with the large, glass-enclosed play ground. For years this corner was inhabited by the Will's family business, where they sold gas at the pump and in bulk. Old Julius Will started the operation following World War II, and when he died in 1953 his son Clarence took over, running the business until fire destroyed it in 1989.

Before Julius built his station, the corner housed a church building of sorts. Not an edifice but a squat structure that snuggled down into the good earth like a toad. The eaves of the roof hung only a couple feet above ground level, just enough for small windows, windows like in most basements, to allow some light into the place. To enter it one descended a staircase.

I suspect that in the eyes of the preacher who held forth there the place was more than a church. It triumphantly signified righteousness' inevitable victory over iniquity, for before the subsurface space was claimed for worship it had been the gathering place of those who drank and danced, the kind of place and gatherings good, god-fearing parents warned their children against. It made no difference that one could get good food there, it was a dark den frequented by those who seemed not to care about the condition of their souls. With those kinds of enticements I suspect the place did well, though during the War it did close down. Perhaps most of its clientele had marched off to war. The place was called, "The Kave."

I was born too late to experience the atmosphere of the place, though I suspiciously viewed it from the outside on occasion. I first descended those forbidden steps to attend an evangelistic service. A young preacher had bustled into town, found the property vacant, and claimed it in the name of God and goodness. He confidently chased out the lingering demons and baptized the place into the Faith, christening it, "The Pipestone Gospel Chapel." We fledgling Evangelicals and Methodists agreed that God was powerfully, and appropriately, at work through the preacher. He was a courageous knight doing battle with our town's darkness. And because he was considerably younger than our ministers, he was a tad more attractive.

Like all wayfaring evangelists before him, he advertised each week in the *County Star*. He was not above buying an occasional eighth-page spread, complete with the obligatory picture of himself, but mostly he advertised with smaller announcements, which included the titles of his Wednesday evening and Sunday morning messages. He unabashedly promised the blessings of God on all who attended. My presence at a meeting was assured after my cousin George secured the eternal salvation of his soul one night in response to the preacher's call to repentance. My mother and Ruby Lessin were quick to decide that their children, Phyllis, Roger, John, and I, could benefit from this man of God who preached salvation in ways that the mainstream churches had either forgotten how to do, or had never known how to in the first place.

We knew several days in advance about the service we would attend, and we were genuinely curious about the title of the message–"Hell: Twenty-five miles from Pipestone." Like the Israelites to whom Amos went, we were curious about which community or den of iniquity had now fallen under God's stern judgment. Twenty-five miles. That was a puzzle. Slayton lay twenty-eight miles to the east. Luverne, twenty-four miles to the south. No community lay precisely twenty-five miles either to the west or to the north. The geography just did not work out. Maybe the preacher advertised in round figures. Anyway, by the night of the service we had exhausted every possibility, which only whet our appetites for discovering upon whom he would call down the wrath of God.

Alas, he proved to be a true Amos, his judgments settling heavily and at last upon we Pipestonians. We were not prepared for that, and his message flattened out our curiosity like a straight pin on a railroad track. We were not scoffers and on another night might have proved attentive, but that evening our ears were hardened to the voice of God. I'm sure mom was disappointed, and yet she gave the preacher one fewer chance than she had given the train engineer years before. Cousin George notwithstanding, we were not taken back for a second try. We would have to live with the curse of being human.

The twenty-five miles he sermonized about did not lead to a neighboring community that was wallowing in its corporate sins, or to a Kave-like enterprise that begged to be closed down, but rather to a place twenty-five miles straight down, the place called Hades. For several days after the meeting we discussed how he came to that information. We had never heard it stated so specifically. Why couldn't it be four miles down. That would be sufficient. Indeed, we became doubters of this man of God. For the sake of a mile or two or ten, the young preacher that night lost any future chances to reel us in.

Chapter Twelve

....

The Raft

One summer the Rock Island Railroad stacked a huge pile of creosote-dipped railroad ties along the tracks. When Roger and I discovered them we decided to borrow a few and transport them to the Dredge to make ourselves a raft. Poling miles up and down the Dredge would be grand adventure. We naïvely raised the issue with our folks only to be told, no, we couldn't do that.

The next morning we banned both their refusals and the word "thievery" from our minds and began the monumental task of getting some of those ties from near the depot, over the three-quarter mile of ground to the creek bridge, without being spotted by the depot agent, parent, or snitching sibling. We developed and followed a plan of action. We sneaked up to the pile from the north, keeping the stack between us and the depot, then carefully selected our first tie. It was all we could do to lift it, but lifted we did, carrying it the length of a house before having to drop it. No problem. We would get it there. We were going to build a raft.

Somehow we wrestled the tie north five blocks, staying on the low, west side of the track grade so no one would spot us from the neighborhood. That left us with the long stretch of open field between the tracks and the Johnson house, now occupied by the Hess family. We located a rope and tried dragging the stubborn thing, but discovered we were not physically up to the task. Because we wanted the raft to be ours and ours alone, we dared not ask for help from the neighborhood kids, or there would not be room enough or time enough to enjoy the vessel ourselves. In the end we rolled the tie the one-hundred yards to Hiawatha Avenue. No one would notice that we were rolling a tie across an open field.

Once we reached the Hesses our problem was less challenging. A deep ditch ran along the quarry road, all the way from Hiawatha to the Dredge. This ditch carried the heavy rains to the creek. We could have used a good rain to float our tie along, but such was not to be. Again, carrying the increasingly stubborn bulk short distances at a time, we managed to push, pull, and roll it to the creek just north of the bridge.

By now our hands and jeans and T-shirts were blackened and reeking of creosote, but luckily the Lessins had a new Bendix automatic wash machine, and Roger's parents were not home. The elegant appliance did not do a bang up job of getting things clean, but we got so dirty every day that some stains on our clothes would not be questioned. Even a variety of oily smells would not raise suspicions. Once redressed, we figured day one was a success.

After a vigorous, three-day crusade we managed to wrestle four of the illegally appropriated, balking, blue–black things down the final slope of the bank of the Dredge. We triumphantly set them side by side on the soft bank and nailed what scraps of wood we could find across their shared surface. This held them together quite nicely. That task completed, we eagerly tried to launch the thing, but could not budge it. We heaved and tugged and grunted and groaned and broke a variety of sticks and branches trying to lever it into the water, but it sat happily anchored in the mud like a sleeping hippo. We finally had to disassemble it, then reassemble it in the water, no easy task as the creek bottom offered poor footing and the ties insisted on drifting downstream. But when you're having fun, no task is impossible.

We did not choose our launch site well. Generations of north-end youth had dropped from the bridge rocks, bricks, and most anything else that would create a splash. A rapids had taken shape over the years. Barely noticeable at high water, at low water one could walk across the creek on the debris. In other words we could not get our raft to the south side of the bridge, which clearly presented the most navigable stretch of water. To the north a hundred yards the creek split into several, small, over grown channels so we also could not raft very far in that direction either.

Undaunted we christened the raft the, "Rock Island Special," and together pushed it into the stream. It easily carried our combined weight and proved to be remarkably stable. Shortly after the christening our parents discovered what we had done. They even came down to inspect the craft and the creek, and realizing that the shallow water offered no dangers, gave their unspoken permission to enjoy ourselves. We spent two, maybe three summer days poling back and forth and up and down our sheltered bit of creek, and made grand pretense of having fun, and reassured each other that our efforts had been worth it, but before long the raft sat abandoned, available to whomever could bully it away from the shore.

The following spring the high water carried the raft away. We never saw it again.

Chapter Thirteen

If You Don't Get it Right,
You Get Change

I collect newspaper items and columns, tearing them from publications while I'm having breakfast or morning coffee in my favorite cafe. The ragged-edged scraps get folded up, no two alike, and are then tossed on the bedroom dresser or the coffee table when I empty my pockets. They accumulate like dust bunnies and poor Norma never knows what to do with them, though she never discards them. Occasionally I gather them up and pile them in my office with the promise that some day I will get them organized. Curiously, when I look at them a second time I often cannot fathom the reason I saved them. A particular state of mind goes with each piece of newsprint and sometimes its hard to get the two back together.

One type of story I save are the accounts of those outwardly, after-the-fact, repentant people who have been caught doing something devious and outrageously illegal, or undeniably immoral. Consistently, the "in" language for these people is that they "made a mistake." Never, "I stole," "I defrauded," "I abused," "I embezzled," but "I made a mistake." Well, anyone can make a mistake, right?

The terms "right" and "wrong?" seem to baffle many people. Even law students take courses in ethics because they have grown up in a world that too little thinks in such categories. But they're fine words. AND, they point to essential concepts.

One Saturday, when I was eleven years old I wanted to attend the matinee at the *Orpheum*, but for reasons I've forgotten, was told I could not go. Also, I was penniless. Undaunted, after dinner I snuck off to find a way to attend anyway. I went through the alleys behind the stores on Main

Street and gathered up some large, cardboard boxes, fitting one inside another until I could manage a half dozen. These I wrestled over to the Hilliard Wholesale Foods warehouse where they bought boxes for two cents apiece, only to discover they were closed on Saturday afternoons. Pondering the situation, I hatched a new plan. I went into the J.C. Penny store, stealthily picked up a baseball cap, removed the price tag, took it to the counter, and asked to return it. I had gotten it as a gift but I really did not like it. No, I didn't have a receipt because, as I said, it was a gift. The suspicious clerk pulled out a form, scribbled some information on it, had me sign it, and forked over ninety-eight cents. Wow! A whole new world opened up in front me. This beat picking up boxes 49 to 1. I not only saw the movie that summer afternoon, but I stuffed myself like never before on candy and popcorn. It seemed prudent not to be found with leftover money jingling in my pocket.

As I left the theatre my cousin Raymond happened along and saw me. Raymond was sixteen, had gotten a summer job in town, and was rooming at our place. At the supper table he asked me about the movie. That led to an interesting conversation between me and the folks that did not end until I explained where I got the money. I could have said, "I sold boxes," but not only was I a lousy liar, but lying to my parents would turn on the guilt process faster than anything else. I might try to avoid the truth, but to lie to them was out of the question.

Part of the dilemma of a life of crime, I discovered, was that I derived pleasure from it. My deviousness had effortlessly produced almost a dollar. Old time tent preachers consistently reminded their audiences that sin abounds because it is so pleasurable, which left we toe-the-line Christians a rather bleak expectation from life—only bland, good times, the kind that boring preachers and their families lived.

Mom and dad knew nothing of karma, but they practiced it anyway. They operated from the premise, "As you sow, so shall you reap." And harvest time fell upon me. By seven o'clock that evening we were back at the counter in J. C. Penny's. The manager was summoned and he and the sales clerk were informed that I had something to tell them. Mom and dad then withdrew, leaving me in that awesomely lonely space that demanded honesty. They stayed within earshot to make sure I got it right. No thought was given to the idea that I had made a mistake. I had stolen the cap, and lied about how it came into my possession. I now had to confront authority, confess my theft, and, alas, make amends. My prized possession at the time was a silver dollar that I kept in an envelop in the top drawer of the dining room buffet. It was not spending money, but rather a collectible. That evening, however, I exchanged it for two copper pennies.

My parents were common, uneducated people. And ethical. If they ever wondered whether they made any contributions to a better world (and I really don't think they thought about it), I would suggest they raised five caring, ethical and moral children. Sometimes I ponder whether my life is making a contribution to the world, and come up with that single claim, that my wife Norma and I have produced five, ethical, caring people to populate our society.

As to the J. C. Penny caper, to my memory, the issue never was raised again by my parents. They probably hoped that my experience was sufficient to instruct me about life and their expectations of me. It did leave me with one lasting impression, however. I conjured up the belief that when people grow into adulthood, they become honest and own up to their failings. One of my disappointments in growing up was to discover that many people walking around in mature bodies were far more "mistake prone" than responsible.

Chapter Fourteen

....

Sleeping Out

As kids we frequently slept outside under the stars. No one had sleeping bags in those days, nor did we crawl into tents. We simply grabbed a pillow and a couple blankets and made beds wherever we decided to spend the night, sometimes out front on what we called the boulevard, other times out back under the clothes lines, this yard, that yard, it really did not matter. The good Earth was soft in those days, the stars bright, unexpected night sounds trustworthy. Not even the crunch of gravel under an unseen foot was cause for alarm.

Typically, only gentle sounds ruffled the quiet of night, even in late summer when crickets found their hind legs and frogs began courting. We delighted in the faint cries of what we called night birds. Though we never saw one, and if put to the test, could not have described one, we knew they were there, flitting about among the stars. So, too, in the distance, always in the distance, occasional steam engines traced the Great Northern rails to wonderful places only dreamed of. Their distinctive, soft-edged cries could not pierce the soft night air, but only float upon it. Of all Earth's generations, only three or four have been romanced by this sound, and no god has offered the poet the gifts necessary to capture the experience for those poor souls denied it.

We slept next to the grass, with its ever changing but always honest aromas, knowing the feel of it through blanket and sprawling arms. Overhead swayed the silhouettes of tree branches, setting the rhythm for the rustling leaves. We must have shared space with exploring spiders, curious mice, and flitting bats, though none of this ever occurred to us. Curiously, I remember no one ever taking on a wood tick. Indeed, I was fourteen before I ever saw one; they seem not to have been part of the landscape in those times.

We discovered that the chill, if we experienced any, came from below, so we would layer two blankets on the ground, with two or three of us bedding down together on top. We would lie there and talk, sometimes serious talk for children, always alert for shooting stars. When we saw one we would shout, "Money, money," the argument being that the first to cry out would soon find some.

We became familiar with the nighttime sky and could even pick out a few of the constellations, other than the two Ursas. In time I learned that "my" star, the one I had chosen as my own and named Clarence, was actually the North Star. During the summer months my bed was on our enclosed porch, along the north wall. The northern sky was my nighttime companion, that and Clarence. I never have been much of a camper, but were I to get disoriented in the wilds at night, I would simply look for the view through the porch window to determine directions.

With our backs to the good earth, and the dark, brilliantly detailed, fabric of nighttime sky hanging over us, the moon could be coyly intimate.

The moon is beautiful
tonight—so white and
round and full.
So alive and close it
beckoned me
to reach out and touch—
I did, and to my
astonishment, . . .
someone giggled.
                                        –RAG

All who have scanned the nighttime sky and wondered are family; the stars form the bridge connecting us each to the other. The landscape evolves, the surging seas alter coast lines, even the mountains slowly change their faces, but the night sky is "forever." The heavens pondered by Cro-Magnon, the African cultures, by Lao Tze and Jesus, Cleopatra and Galileo, Lincoln, granddad and aunt Emma has been the same sky. Assurance rests in that awareness. When we feel frazzled and crave a sense of stability in this raging world, it is time to sleep out under the stars.

I noticed last night that the neighbors across the way have put in a blazing yard light. Their house, garage, garden and trees, the parked Ford, all were bathed in not unpleasant, though intrusive, light. I understand. Outdoor lights are going up in pace with our growing sense of vulnerability. A small handful of separated individuals are stealing the blessed darkness from us, causing the stars to retreat into the lightened sky even as people retreat into the inner sanctuaries of their homes. Do the pilferers and thieves have any sense of the magnitude of their acts? We magnify their typically paltry power by the energy of our fears, and I suspect some of them feed on that. And as the violence escalates, more lights will go up. At this point Norma and I agree: we are not willing to yield the stars to them.

Chapter Fifteen

....

Reggie

One year Inez Clarksean shouldered the heavy load of teaching a split class, half fifth graders, half sixth graders. I was of the second category. I vaguely remember her appearance, and have a few recollections of happenings in her classroom, and one vividly clear picture from the second week of April, 1946.

Upon arrival at school that morning we all heard that Reggie Krumm had been killed the evening before over by the water tower. Returning home from a friend's house, he had dashed into the street behind a passing pickup truck without seeing the loaded grain trailer being pulled behind. He was run over, and died at the hospital thirty minutes later. We learned the details in fragments, each new piece of information giving birth to additional unanswerable questions.

We students gathered around Miss Clarksean's desk that morning, participating in the most adult conversation of our young lives. Most of us had known old people who died, and had seen death portrayed in multiplied numbers of movies, but never had most of us known of someone our age who had died or been killed. It felt unnatural, and life suddenly felt uncertain.

Not everyone in class knew Reggie (he was two-three grades below us in school), but everyone focused on his death. I knew him as the neatly dressed, little, boy who played on the sidewalk in front of the Red and White grocery store where my mother worked. Reggie seemed always to be clean. I attributed this to his having no trees to climb, no gardens to dig in, no Dredge to play along. Reggie's neatness was emphasized by his almost white hair and fair complexion. My mother knew him as the nice, little boy who came to the store on errands for his parents, who lived in the apartment above *Hirmer's Meat Market.*

In our discussion at Miss Clarksean's desk we were told that we would probably be able to see Reggie at the Funeral Home by the following day. Some of my classmates seemed ready to do so; I was not at all sure I wanted to.

The 1940's provided schoolchildren something that is now long gone—an hour and fifteen minute noon break. The farm students and a few town students brown-bagged their lunch, but many others, including me, went home for dinner (lunch). At break I would hurry to *Dibble's Chevrolet Garage,* where dad was a mechanic, and catch a ride home with him. Following dinner I would return to school by foot or bike, both requiring me to hurry.

On April 10, 1946 I was trotting the last few blocks to school when I met three eighth-grade girls coming out of the Walz Funeral Home. They had been to see Reggie. Yes, I could do so too. Just walk in.

Classes were about to start, but I could not resist doing what I really did not want to do. The home and situation beckoned me. I walked up the front steps and entered the glass-paneled door. Before me an open staircase rose to the second floor where the Walz family, where Bobby Walz, a classmate, actually lived. To the left an open archway invited me into the funeral parlor. I cautiously approached, then stepped into its gloomy recess, much aware of the cushion of thick carpeting beneath my feet. Something inside me became heavy as I realized I was alone in the room.

I shifted my gaze around the dimly lit space, allowing my eyes to adjust to the relative darkness, then hesitantly brought it to rest on the lighted casket at the front of the room. Reggie's nose and part of his face was visible above the edge of the satin-lined casket. I slowly approached, bumping into a metal chair that scandalously banged up against another. Suddenly unsure of myself, I looked back toward the entrance. No one appeared to question my irreverent presence.

Shortly I stood before the unwelcome mystery. Reggie had always been of fair complexion but now he was even more pale. So this was death? I looked at his chest. It was still. I reminded myself that the breath was gone, that it would never return. That soon Reggie would be placed in the silent darkness of the ground to remain there forever. All alone.

Suddenly I was falling through a cold, vast, dark space, end over end, falling, falling. This great, yawning emptiness was within me. I felt cold all over. Jerking myself around I hurried out of the building, silently rejoicing in the spring warmth and sunshine that greeted me at the front steps. The empty feeling shortly dissipated, returning in a lesser form only one more time that afternoon. I never told another person that I had gone to see Reggie, and consequently did not share my reaction to the experience either.

On a spring afternoon in 1978 I was driving through south Minneapolis. As I rounded a corner the funeral sign on the building across the intersection caught my eye and in that instant I was tumbling once again through that vast, cold emptiness. I did not remember, but rather was unwillingly transported back to that lonely, cushioned sanctum of thirty-two years before. I was eleven years old, standing uncertainly before the reality of death. The inner transformation was short lived, though powerful. How curious. As a minster I have often been witness to the awesome mystery of someone's final breath, and of course have officiated at many funerals. Still, there silently resides within me a twelve-year old and his unexplored, unexamined confrontation with death.

Chapter Sixteen

Earth's Superiority

I've never met a Biblical literalist, though I've met many people who staunchly asserted to be one. I've even met a few who insist the Bible contains, not the Word of God, but the words of God. Of course, it's just a game people play, and even the most literal of believers picks and chooses what will be claimed as the "inerrant Word," and virtually always "The Word" is one that works for that person. We all write our own Bibles. To keep religion intellectually honest requires continual self-examination, and none of us is sufficiently overflowing with integrity or self-awareness to make it work well. In the end all religion is illusion, in both the productive and the unproductive sense of the word. As many ministers learn, in preaching the power is not in the *logos*, but in the *mythos*. Translated: give the people what they want to hear. I never was very good at that.

As children most of us were raised with the literalist's view of the Bible. God created the world in six days, and when the end of time was visited upon us the New Jerusalem would come down out of heaven, a gigantic cube (though that was never emphasized). It's foundations of precious gems supporting sturdy walls of stone (to keep the unworthy out), its gates of pearl and streets of gold were "gospel," and a description that always left me yearning for something softer. New Jerusalem's inhabitants would be cursed with the experience of Midas, never to experience the varieties and textures of life. And I asked, "Where are the birds?" "Where are the trees for them to nest in?" Even a child understood that an existence devoid of green branches and bird song fell short of being a heaven.

We Northenders of the thirties and forties had birds and trees and butterflies; we were several steps up on heaven. Even so, we were much poorer in such matters than we realized. Each fall our schoolteachers would encourage us to celebrate the glorious colors of autumn, and so we would, all the brilliant browns and wasted yellows. Alas, on the north end we were surrounded by those trees that typically die without bold statement—boisterous box elders, effusive elms, cloying cottonwoods. Only the willows made any pretence of being excited about going into hibernation. South of the tracks an occasional oak or maple may have been established, but if so, I never saw one. Still, the smell and feel and delightful crunch of fall were sufficient to generate those senses that make autumn the darling of the seasons. This wondrous time needs no carnival atmosphere to make it special, and we were satisfied.

What was true of trees repeated itself among the birds; we knew but few of the feathered families; but each one we knew, of course, was special. For instance, sparrows will ever enjoy a favored place in my heart, for they were the faithful birds of all seasons. These little creatures, molded by the milder clime of the British Isles, none-the-less did not desert us in the short days of winter.

In my teens my bedroom window looked out over the roof of the front porch. The peak of the roof ran right up under the windowsill and was capped by a galvanized tube. Inside this metal cylinder, that must have been brutally cold in winter, families of sparrows nested. Mornings and afternoons they would hop about on the roof, finding cause to chirp their best at the season's worst. The identical roofline and circumstance also existed outside the west window. I grew to love the sparrows. For whatever reason, the place I now live seldom exhibits one of these little creatures. We have a large and wonderful variety of blue, red, and multicolored birds that frequent our winter and summer feeders, but only seldom will a sparrow brighten the place up, and I miss them.

Besides the humble sparrows we also had that fair weather harbinger of spring, the robin. Upon seeing the first brick-red belly of the season we each were scripted to say, "Spring is here." Robins, of course, are the winged curse of those who like to grow fruit. They particularly like berries, and manage often to beat the gardener by a few slim hours to the harvest.

Following worship one summer morning dad and I walked into the back yard. Across the woven fence sat Fred Stolte, our longtime, good neighbor. Fred was in his late seventies at the time, straight and sturdy in spite of his many years. He held a BB gun in his lap and he was fighting back tears. His tears were of frustration because the robins were taking his strawberry harvest, but also his were tears of sorrow. He motioned us to come around to the gate and into the back yard. He directed us to look into the oil drum he used for a burn barrel, which we did. It was a third full with the bodies of robins. He had been shooting them all morning, but they just kept coming, and he was the hapless victim, fighting to save his berries and of having to kill the birds to do it. And the killing was for naught; in the end the robins won. Still, these birds were a generally appreciated part of the summer landscape.

The most welcome springtime arrival was the meadowlark. God gifted no bird with a more melodious song. People of the wooded hills might think the world of meadow and field to be barren, but without them we might not have the larks. These brown and yellow birds consistently pick the most conspicuous spots from which to sing. During the war years they were the most patriotic of birds. They would proudly present the black V on their chest and encourage us with their special song: *V-for-vic-tory-meadowlark.*

We had an abundance of the beautiful pheasant that was mercilessly hunted each fall. And although they were drastically down in numbers, on a fall night one could go out in the yard and just maybe hear a flock of geese go over in the darkness, honking their encouragement to one another. The geese brought out the same kind of response as did private air planes. When a *Piper Cub* flew over people came out of their houses to watch. And in the case of the geese, to listen. Though now abundant, I still pause in spiritual stillness as a flock of these noble birds pass over.

We were taught to disdain what my older siblings called *Butcher Birds,* believing them to be nest robbers. Whether it was a shrike or a kingbird that we were looking at, I don't know, but they could put on quite a show when excited.

Glorious redheaded woodpeckers were abundant in those days, their colors as vibrant and distinctive as the song of the meadowlark. These wonderful birds are struggling to survive the competition for habitat in today's environment.

One other bird of my youth must be mentioned—the intelligent, shy, and gregarious crow. In recent years these birds have moved into the towns and cities, and although still shy, have, to some extent, lost their cautious ways. They are among the most interesting birds that come to our feeding stations. They are scavengers, carrying off most anything to eat or store away. They will even take a dried biscuit, hop up onto the birdbath, dunk the biscuit to soften it up, and then fly off with the prize. Remarkable.

The crow's intelligence is widely heralded, and when I was small everyone knew that apocryphal person who split the tongue of a crow so it could talk like a parrot. Somewhere in his book, *African Genesis,* Robert Ardrey describes how older crows teach the young of the flock about hunters. Without ever being shot at, adolescent crows learn which particular humans to avoid because they are the killers.

In the rural area many considered crows a nuisance, and because they were so wily and such a challenge with their habit of posting sentry birds whenever they fed or roosted, many hunted them. So, too, the educated knew crows could count to three. If three hunters went into a grove of trees, three better come out or the crow would go nowhere near the spot. However, if four hunters went in and three came out, these "stupid" birds could be fooled.

Crows hate owls and hawks, and no better decoy was possible than staking a stuffed or fake owl over the body of a crow. The birds would raise the alarm and their calls would bring their kind in from every direction. They would become so furious over the sight of an owl with a crow kill that they would throw their normally cautionary ways to the winds and circle and repeatedly swoop down upon the lifeless enemy, thus coming blindly into gun range of waiting hunters. Among humans, we call this the game of "Seduction"–draw them in, then zap them. I've seen the game played viciously and with tragic results. For the crow, too.

These black flocks gone berserk often resulted in their members dead and piled up in front of hunters for the obligatory photo session. Pictures never were taken when the hunters came back empty-handed, but few opportunities to verify their killing prowess were neglected when they didn't. They seemed not to recognize that the "glory" of the kill falls far short of the true glory of a living creature. Of course, the photos were all about ego. This remains one of the least attractive attributes of the human family, and stands as a ready reminder that the Kingdom is not yet at hand. I embrace *Isaiah's* claim that when the human family comes to the knowledge of God, all such violence will cease. Our murderous ways testify against us.

Still, Heaven, as described by the unknown John in the Revelation, falls far short of Earth's grandeur. What better reason to read our Scriptures with a critical eye.

Chapter Seventeen

....

The Happy Mediums

Virtually everyone of my generation can sing the *Cream of Wheat* song.

Cream of Wheat is so good to eat that we have it every day.
We sing this song, it will make us strong, and it makes us shout "hooray."
It's good for growing babies and grown-ups too to eat,
For all the family's breakfast you can't beat Cream of Wheat.

Except for the mothers who had grander designs for their children's lives and sent them to piano practice on Saturday mornings, the rest of us learned this jingle because it introduced our Saturday morning passion, *Let's Pretend*. Each Saturday we pre-teens would gather around our Motorolas or Philcos to hear Nila Mack's troop, including Miriam Wolfe, Marilyn Erskine, and Bill Lipton, dramatize a fairy tale, direct from New York. Our imaginations were stirred, good predictably won out over evil, and all felt right with the world. And wonderful Cream of Wheat, whatever it was, made it possible.

The persistent gift of good feelings presented by the entertainment world back then contrasts sharply with the Mediums' offerings today. We were not, of course, so discriminating as today's audiences; some would brand us as simple and naive; and indeed when I listen to old tapes of radio programs, I'm aware that we were easily satisfied. AND, that we were nurtured. Drs. Christian and Malone, Ma Perkins, Perry Mason, Judy Canova, Bob Hope, the Aldrich Family, even the Lone Ranger and the *FBI in Peace and War* gave us a world that was in balance, basically good and reasonable. Even trustworthy. We safely visited 79 Wistful Vista with *Fibber McGee and*

Molly, and even in the shadows with *The Whistler* we knew we had nothing to fear.

The movies were similar. Our lives were subtly influenced by generally gentle plots, often by musicals, and always with endings of virtue triumphing over evil. Indeed, a they-lived-happily-ever-after triteness warmed our foolish hearts like hot cocoa on a winter day. The wholesome June Allison and Van Johnson taught us about basic goodness, while June Haver and Lon McCallister modeled the gentle joy of living. Randolph Scott stood for right and justice, Gary Cooper for courage, and Hope and Crosby and Abbott and Costello for healthy laughter. We had Boris Karloff and Sidney Greenstreet to scare us and the marvelously intense Walter Brennan–whose voice and grimace filled even the ifs, ands, and buts, with emotion–to stir us. We journeyed down river on the *African Queen* and the *Show Boat*, met Judy Garland and Margaret O'Brien in St. Louis, and had our fantasies stirred by *King Kong* and *The Wizard of Oz*. We paid homage to mama and green valleys. *Bambi* and *Dumbo* and *The Yearling* sensitized us, and *Gone With the Wind* hinted that we were taking on sophistication.

On the giant screen love was more romantic than sexual, and sexuality was more a nine-letter word than a three-letter one, and even when intimacy was implied, it was done by curtains softly blowing in the wind or waves washing up on a beach. The distinctions between modesty and blatancy, revelation and exposure, honesty and cynicism were inserted into our thinking. We marched in the *Easter Parade* and danced in the rain, and found a comfortable *Home in Indiana*. And with the rarest of exceptions, we were sent home feeling good. And the exceptions, like *The Ox Bow Incident*, sent us home with important values to weigh. It was a meat and potatoes fare. Was it unrealistic? Of course it was; and it was a wonderful antidote to the general grind of reality that many people lived with. The entertainment industry created soft edges and rounded corners and repeatedly stroked our better instincts to life. And because it happened coast-to-coast and border-to-border, it was no small accomplishment.

Chapter Eighteen

....

Seining Minnows

I wish my dad had gained more education. He deserved that. With more learning under his belt he maybe would not have had to work so hard all his life. He grew up in tobacco country in Kentucky, and even though he finished the third grade he often was held out of class to work in the fields. That was the way of life then. Still, had life dealt differently with him he may not have been the success he was as a father. I speak of him as my dad with great pride. Reincarnationists tell us we choose the parents we want to be born to. If that is true, I chose wisely.

Years ago I read a study done in California on stimulating students to do their homework. They discovered that the number one incentive to get students to study was the promise of ten, uninterrupted minutes each week with their dads. Wow! During an era when people worked six days a week, and often ten or more hours a day, dad spent a great deal of time with me, and I assume with my older siblings (I need to ask them about that). Spring and summer we got out the gloves and played catch after supper. On cold winter nights I sat on his lap as he chatted with company or studied the pictures in *Life* or *Look* magazines. Together we listened to the Lone Ranger, or raked the lawn, or practiced casting with rod and reel.

On summer, Sunday mornings we sat on the front porch steps together, polishing our shoes in preparation for Sunday School and Church. As we waxed and buffed we talked of many things. For instance, a magnificent boxelder tree shaded our front yard. Its special feature, other than its size, was a huge, log-like branch that stretched horizontally south. In very obliging fashion (this was a very friendly tree), the one branch became two firm arms forming a comfortable cradle—you sat on one limb and leaned back against the other, your bottom hanging not-at-all precariously in space.

This couch seven feet above the ground accommodated three, and I and friends whiled away many summer hours in the mottled shade there, eating green apples or just "hanging out." Alone, I would lounge there to read a book.

One Sunday morning over our polishing, dad and I decided to count the leaves on this giant friend, just out of curiosity, for we had no idea how many leaves a tree held. We decided to select a representative branch, count the leaves on that, and then multiply that figure by the number of other similar branches, deducting or adding-to, depending on their size. We shortly discovered that short of severing one from the tree we could not count the leaves on a single branch; nor did the tree sport a truly representative branch; and because of its grand proportions, branches had branches and . . . . The old tree was just too big. Our quick failure was not important, however, but the merging of our minds in speculation was.

Together we celebrated the world around us. In earlier years, when dad still worked the long hours, we did most of our fishing at Lake Shetek, along the dike leading to Vahalla Island, a destination conveniently manageable in an evening or on a Sunday afternoon. Lake Shetek was nine miles long, and at its deepest, 18 feet. Like many prairie lakes it slowly was filling in with silt. On more than one occasion we pondered how long it would take to empty the lake a thimbleful of water at a time. Or a cupful at a time. Or how much the level of the lake would drop with the removal of a single cup of water, and whether that one less cup of water could be distributed over the entire surface, and if not, where would its absence be noticed. We never had answers, of course, but the delight was in the questions.

The joy elicited by questions remains with me still. Although I've spent most of my adult life as a minister, I've never been a religious person. I don't like religion. I don't like what religion does to the Christian Faith, and following all that, I've never been much interested in religious answers. It's the questions that quicken life. Spiritual hunger is a fire that must be fed, a fire that's never satisfied, a fire that never says "enough." Questions are the fuel, answers more like the ash, and the seemingly unlimited number of possible questions keeps a living faith vital and worthwhile. You trust the love and patience of God, and ask away, always exploring. That's an approach to life I began learning while polishing shoes on summer, Sunday mornings.

Dad still visits me. Not in person, he's been gone now several years, but in spirit. For instance, he was with me this past week as I determined that the various congregations of birds that worship at our summer feeders, eat and kick out approximately 61,000 seeds a day. My carefully produced estimate, accomplished by counting the number of seeds in a quarter-cup measure, then converting the quarter-cup count into the quart count, *etc.*, provided me not only with an answer, but with cause to appreciate and celebrate Mother Earth's task in feeding her children, and how marvelously well she does it. So it is, that simple questions lead to spiritual awarenesses.

Dad and I never let right answers assume importance in our arguments, and in my adolescent years we argued incessantly. I usually initiated the fuss, and we would go at it over most any issue, neither one of us knowing what we were talking about. I loved it. I needed it. One of my regrets is that I never told dad how important these mental tugs of war were to me. He maybe experienced his son simply as a rebellious, bullheaded, adolescent, one not above becoming obnoxious on occasion, but for me the debates were wonderful wrestling matches with my dad. When I became too big to sit on his lap, too old to be carried piggyback across a field, then these verbal fights became intimate exchanges, a way of having closeness with him that I knew no other way to experience.

I mentioned dad spending time with picture magazines. He could struggle through a Western pulp magazine, and did so on winter evenings, but beyond that he read little; most of his learning came through studying pictures. Sitting on his lap I would get totally bored as he spent endless minutes examining photographs in magazines. In time I learned he was schooling himself. As one who has learned that even stones offer unending revelations if you spend time with them, I now appreciate his process.

I once heard a 33 year-old man wail to his dead father, "You went and died, and never gave me your blessing." It was like Esau crying out to his father Isaac, "Don't you have a blessing for me too, father." Each son, I will not presume to speak for daughters, has this awesome need for his father's blessing. I occasionally find opportunity to remind fathers of how important that is. You must find a way to give your children your blessing before you die. How lucky I was. Dad repeatedly gave me his. Mostly through sharing time with me. (I almost said, "spending time with me," but it was more than that. It was truly time shared). He also gave me his verbal blessing when I was twenty-seven years old, with a wife and four children to support. I was contemplating leaving my job to attend college, and in time, seminary. I had no money. Dad said to me, "Son, I believe that is what God intends for you. And if that is so, you can do it."

Do you hear the blessing? It's not so much in the encouragement, important as that was, but in his use of the word, "son." Not everyone will know what I'm saying, some will. "Son," as a form of address, can be powerfully intimate. I know fathers who address their sons as "boy," which to my ears always has distance built into it, and at best feels like a slap on the shoulder. It has only one hand. Most fathers use their sons' names in addressing them. My dad did. But "son" as a form of address carries with it all those unspoken mysteries of blood-of-my-blood, bone-of-my-bone, spirit-of-my-spirit kinds of things. The word "son" is a two-handed, two-armed embrace.

I've often pondered that within White Western culture a mother has no equivalent, powerful way to address her daughter. At least I'm not aware of any. Among African Americans you hear "girl" warmly used that way, and that maybe comes closest, though it is a more commonly used form of address than "son." Perhaps because men are more uncomfortable with such soft words.

Only once did I ever hear my dad address my brother Kenny with that special word, but when I heard it, I knew. As a nine-year-old I recognized something very substantial and significant had just happened. Dad was reaching in and reaching out with all the love that the father-son connection generates. Kenny was home on the furlough that preceded his being shipped overseas. I don't remember what he said to my mother in a joking fashion, maybe something about coming back in a box or something of that nature. Whatever he said, it caused mother to cry, and she typically did not. And at that uncomfortable, poignant moment dad chose to use "the word." He said, "Son, please don't talk like that; it hurts your mother." A special word on a special occasion to simultaneously chastise the action and reaffirm and draw upon the unbreakable bond. Dad could have said anything, and with the inclusion of the word "son," it would have been a statement of love. That was Kenny's one time (that I know of). Mine was in the exchange above.

How proud I've always been to be my father's son. How assuring to hear that vital relationship affirmed in a word, a word that offered blessing in its expression. I use that word very cautiously as a form of address; indeed, I can tell you exactly how many times I've used it with each of my three sons. What I'm saying is that dad consistently offered blessing, that he always was there, to play catch, to practice our softball pitching, to fish, to hunt, to argue, to fetch me when the car ran out of gas, to pull me out of a snow-bank. He was my dad. I was his son.

Together the two of us repeatedly played out a parable of what a father-son relationship is meant to be: we seined minnows together. Indeed, one of the joys of my life as a boy in western Minnesota in the forties and early fifties was the frequent Saturday evening trip to Bill Farmer's to do so. When my brother Kenny entered the Army Air Corps in forty-three, I became dad's partner in getting the bait for the frequent fishing trips. Scrawny, inadequate-to-the-task, me.

Our twenty-foot seining net hung along the outside, north wall of the garage like some great macrame piece, placed there to dry after the last trip to Bill Farmer's pasture. The net had poles attached to each end and using these we would lift it from the wall and roll it up, both ends to the middle. It was my job to place it on the front bumper of our 36 *Terraplane*. (When I explain this to my grandchildren it is hard for them to picture, bumpers being what they are today, but in those times a bumper was a substantial piece of steel that stuck out far enough in front of the car to do some good. And it formed an effective cradle for the rolled-up net.) We took a common minnow bucket along to transport the minnows home.

Bill Farmer's was one of my special places. I introduced high school friends to it, and we went there often, and I could hardly wait to share it with Norma when I began dating her. The beauty of the place, of course, was all within me, though she pretended to be impressed. A more ordinary, less attractive place would be hard to conjure up. But it was at Bill Farmer's that significant instances of my life happened. For instance, it was in that creek that dad tried to teach me to swim. The entire family was there, frolicking around in the water. I was four or five. Dad had on one of those silly swimsuits of a bygone era; a one-piece, black cotton affair with bib and shoulder straps. Its stylish cut was highlighted with a large, round hole on each side just above the hip. Dad carried me out into the water, cradled me in his arms and lowered me into the water, telling me to stroke and kick. Terrified, I could only scream and cry. Finally mother intervened and told him to take me back to shore.

To get into Farmer's pasture you drove along the Milwaukee Road right-of-way, all the way to the trestle. The trestle was quite ordinary, made of timbers, and carrying trains perhaps ten-twelve feet above Pipestone Creek. Dad would pick me up and safely carry me over. How I admired his expertise. But the day came, of course, when I was big enough to try it myself. I hung onto the rail with both hands and took uncertain sidesteps from one tie to the next, fully aware of the yawning emptiness below. It was slow going and more than once I was rescued from my tedious labor before getting to the other end. But in time, I was walking across it with, "Look, ma, no hands," assurance. That happened at Farmer's.

As a teen-ager I frequently went there plinking with a 22 rifle. On occasion a whole carload came with our guns. We threw cans into the creek and shot them full of holes until they sank. In the winter we hunted cottontails in the open pastureland. One fall, alone, I came with my 410 shotgun, and when a big bird rose up out of the marsh, what dad called a "shypoke," I raised my gun and fired. The big bird cartwheeled out of the air onto the ice of the creek, its wing shattered. Suddenly filled with remorse over my unthinking act, I ran over to end its suffering. I used the butt-end of the gun to beat the poor thing's head. On about the third stomp the gun fired and blew off the tip of the bill off my cap. That was part of my history at Bill Farmer's.

The most remarkable thing about Bill Farmer's is that his cattle always grazed there, and we adolescents were almost always with gun, but not once did Bill ever come down to chase us off or tell us to put away our firearms. And to my knowledge, no animal was ever hurt.

The land at Farmer's was flat and the creek took its own time meandering through his place, turning back on itself time and again like syrup being poured from a bottle. Because of occasional steep banks we could not seine just anywhere, but lots of stream was available within a short walk because of its ambling nature.

The mechanics involved in seining were simple enough if only we kept the bottom edge of the net—which was weighted with lead—dragging along the stream-bed. That was the minnow's best avenue of escape. The top of the net had a series of wooden floats to keep the upper edge on or near the surface. Dragging the net required a truly coordinated effort, with both of us tugging and pulling evenly as we sloshed along, sometimes with feet sucked into the mud, sometimes floundering on slippery footing, but never stopping. The act could even produce drama. The one time I remember dad using a four-letter word occurred when, struggling in knee-deep mud, he lost his balance and wound up sitting down into the sticky goo. "Shit," he said, as his pole and his end of the net floated beyond him down stream. The world sucked in its breath ever so slightly at the untypical exclamation. And I was of little help to him because I could not stop laughing.

I recently asked my brother if he could remember dad cursing. After a bit of thought he said, yes, once. When President Kennedy was assassinated. The rumor was rampant that Lyndon Johnson was behind the killing and evidently dad bought into it. According to Kenny, that drew a, "That goddamned Johnson," from him.

Seining minnows is kin to feeding a slot machine; you must invest something to win, but you also might lose. However, the odds at Farmer's were heavily weighted in favor of a win. On an average evening three pulls produced all the minnows we wanted, and I remember once getting more minnows than we needed in one pull. We always pulled the net against the current. Anyone who has not leaned into a pole, tugging a net upstream, probably cannot understand how something that is almost totally composed of holes can pull so hard through the water. But it does. And dad and I would pull together, tugging, groaning, slogging along, until we could drag up onto a beach or sandbar. This, of course, was an act filled with anticipation as we eagerly spread the net to see what the pull had produced. In certain seasons the catch might consist of nothing but crayfish, but more usually a wide variety of small fish were trapped. The luckily unattractive, dull-colored or unstreamlined fish (our judgment), the carp, stone-rollers, sunfish, crayfish, and all unidentified types, went back into the water. Chubs, shiners, and at times, suckers, became the victims of our whim, destined to be helplessly skewered on a fish hook, like unnumbered minnows before them, and not unlike the untold billions of worms that have squirmed and contracted their remarkable bodies in their attempts to escape being impaled in the same way; fruitlessly, like butterflies in the hands of a pin-wielding youngster. As I said before, we lived by the strange notion that "being" can be owned, most especially if it comes with cold blood and scales, or an elongated body that pursues its wonderfully creative task out of sight under the ground.

I always disliked the trip back to the car after the seining. By then we were hot and tired, the rolled net dripping wet and heavy, the minnow pail no longer empty. I carried the bucket, and for several years that was a real struggle; I was too short and too weak to keep it off the ground. My pride was entangled in this struggle, and I would wrap both hands around the handle, walk backwards, now carrying, now dragging it, all the while keeping a lookout for fresh cow pies. Dad would allow this battle to be waged, but before I was utterly defeated he would throw the wet net over one shoulder, pick up the pail with the other, and urge me on ahead.

Once we arrived home the minnows were quickly carried to the basement and emptied into a wooden, nail keg near the floor drain. We kept water trickling into the burlap-draped keg to keep the minnows alive until we had need of them. Then back outside to retrieve the net from the front bumper, to unroll it and return it to the garage wall.

Then came the best part of all. Our ritual. We climbed back into the Terraplane and drove to *Spotty's Drive-In* for double-dipped, chocolate-chip ice cream cones. And then sat in the car in the semidarkness, nursed our cones, and in between licks spoke of those things good men talk about when they get together in quiet places.

Chapter Nineteen

....

Hankie

One golden, summer day I determinedly helped mom shuck the bushel basket of sweet corn that she had lugged in from the garden. I'm sure I did little to empty the basket. Some ears still had the stem protruding and I lacked the strength in my grip and in my wrists necessary to wrench the two apart. These I put into mom's capable, strong hands to snap. I did manage to worry the wrappings off a few ears, however, gouging more than a few tender kernels with my prying fingers as I tried to get the silk out from between the rows of yellow.

Corn is like everything else that grows. Some ears are fully formed, others not. And a few are malformed. But they're all corn. Holding up an ear that was half kernel, half cob, I asked mom why such should be. She answered out of that small collection of quasi-answers with which every parent must be armed to handle the constant stream of that most profound of questions, "Why?"

"That's just the way it is."

Even for a six-year-old that was not totally satisfying, and yet it was internalized as the only answer available. With some things, "That's just the way it is." For instance, my dog totally grosses me out when he scarfs up some smelly, decaying piece of mouse flesh left behind by the mower, as though he had a grand prize. At such times Norma is my mentor as she reminds me, "That's just what dogs do." I guess mom's answer was not as evasive as I've sometimes thought. Often wisdom's way is just accepting what is. Or acknowledging, "I don't know."

The far North End embraced an individual who was not unlike the ear of corn I held up for examination that August morning. In him "the ear never filled out," either physically or mentally. And paradoxically, this uncomplicated man had a beautiful wholeness about him; his mind and body went together and seemed always to be present. He was one of us, and to everyone he was known simply, even affectionately, as *Hankie.*

Hankie was a dozen years older than I, a short man who usually wore bibbed overalls. His body never grew properly, in a horizontal sort of way. One half of his body could walk straight ahead, but had to tug along the other half that tended to go off to the side. He got around just fine that way, though running was not a smooth process for him. Nor speaking. Hankie always enjoyed the attention of others and had a shy way of looking pleased when you talked to him. He could carry on simple conversation, though vowels seemed to linger in his mouth longer than for other people. Still, the mind, body, and soul of Hankie was balanced and in harmony with his surroundings. He blended in, and almost everyone liked him.

All of this was true, *and* I imagine the void in his life as awesome. He never knew female companionship, never knew much of gentle, human touch. I once met a chiropractor from a rural, Minnesota town who estimated that 85% of his business was from farmers just needing to be touched. In his own way he was a professional prostitute, meeting some basic, human needs. When our house cat experiences stroke hunger she pesters someone until she gets the needed attention. Humans with stroke hunger go to the local chiropractor or the city prostitute. To my knowledge, life offered Hankie neither option. It's possible that when he wound up in the Good Samaritan Home in his later years he received some catch-up touching. I hope so (Good Samaritan was/is located in the former Reservation School).

Hankie and his family lived across the road from us in a two-room house, and so I saw him often, though because of the age difference I did not spend time with him. I don't know how he filled many of his hours, but I often saw him walking Second Avenue towards town or on a return trip, and he did go to movies on occasion. He also did chores around their place. For instance, in the fall he would dig potatoes, turning the rich, black soil with a potato fork, picking up the reds and whites in a slow but tireless fashion.

Hankie also enjoyed fishing, and his brother would occasionally take him bull-heading up at Lake Benton. Hankie could skin a bullhead with the best of them.

He never attended school. In today's world, with the special help available, he may have blossomed more fully than he did then. He never was given the chance, however. I have no idea what Hankie's inner life was like? Did he define himself, as many of us do, by his limitations? Or was he too wise for that? His accomplishments, given his gifts, were probably equal to mine, but what of his dreams? How high did he reach in his fantasies?

What regrets settled on him with the passing years? Most of mine fall into the category of wishing I had risked more. I wonder, do dreams get bigger or smaller with personal limitations? Did Hankie possess the good sense to simply enjoy each moment, each day? How did this special child of God experience God? Did Hankie ever pray? Did he need to? Perhaps, like a child, he was prayer. If the gods were to offer me gifts, one request might be to go back and spend some time with Hankie, to explore as best I could the spirit of the man, and to share with him what we know and sense in common. To be his friend.

For many of the years that I knew him Hankie's constant companion was his gentle, orange and white, shorthaired dog, "Barney." Only one time in all those years did I ever see Hankie become angry. I don't remember how it developed, but Barney was under Stolte's porch (we and the Stolte's shared a common, double, driveway), and because one of the older neighborhood kids was lobbing rocks at him, Barney was cowering in the partial gloom at the far end of the crawlspace. When Hankie saw that Barney was being abused he pulled out his pocketknife, opened it, and went after Barney's tormentor, saying, "I'll kill yo-o-u-u!" Poor Hankie was easily eluded but he did stand up for his dog, the thing I so miserably failed to do in my time. Whatever love filled Hankie's life, a large part of it was for his pal Barney.

I cherish one memory of Hankie above all others. It's the day he walked through our yard towards home, dangling a large northern pike on a stringer. He had been fishing at the quarry. We neighborhood kids, we were perhaps 14-15 years old, got all excited about it and asked him to wait until we could weigh it. I ran to the basement and fumbled around in a tackle box until I found a fish scale, and hurried back out into the bright morning light. The northern weighed in at an even twelve pounds. Amidst our oohs, aahs, and wows, Hankie matter-of-factly said, "I caught a bigger one yesterday." The way he said it we knew it was true, and he remained the center of satisfying attention for a few moments longer. Once we determined that he caught both of them on daredevils, we were on our way to the quarry, fishing tackle in hand. In quick succession we caught several northerns that morning, the largest weighing five pounds, but nothing to compare with Hankie's two catches. The quarry was not large enough to house too many big fish, and in wise compassion the quarry carefully selected to whom it yielded its prizes. I suspect Hankie had too few moments of feeling special, though on that fresh, summer morning, I think, he did.

Over the decades I've sporadically thought about Hankie, and a few years ago stopped by the home to see him, only to discover that he had died shortly before.

Chapter Twenty

Saturday Night

Saturday. The Seventh Day. The Sabbath. The day of renewal and rest. The time to reconnect with family and nature. The time, yippee, to be a teenager.

By "Saturday" I really mean, *Saturday Night*, and the preparation for it. This magical event I viewed as a too-young-to-participate bystander, and by the time I was ready to partake, the doors were closing. Some time after the big war the local Chamber of Commerce decided to move Saturday to Friday, so to speak, *ie.*, the stores would be open Friday evenings, closed Saturday evenings. At that precise moment the world developed a hitch in its stride, farmers didn't know when to take their weekly baths, and ever after the once robust weekends routinely limped to their conclusions.

For me Saturday night (small "n") meant mom worked until ten or later at the Red and White store and dad and I made our way to the State Theatre to see the current double feature. Dad's treat. At the time, I received ten-cents a week allowance, which was the price of a movie ticket, and had Dad not treated I would have been penniless most of the time. As it was, I once saved a full $1.95, a feat I have struggled to duplicate ever since.

Time spent with my dad always was special and I still can resurface the proud feeling that accompanied coming out of Marsh's Clothing on a cold, snowy, Saturday night, and standing at the First National Bank curb waiting to cross the street, because I stood there with a cap on my head just like my dad's. I felt five feet tall. We were, of course, on our way to the State.

What the seventh day involved for the teenager I learned from observing my silly sisters. For them Saturday Nights were not marks on a calendar, but events of the soul, and Saturday mornings (and afternoons) were the ritual of preparation. One could not walk into the uncertainty of the Night unprepared, for it could be a minefield of ecstasy, heartbreak, and everything in between. Yeah, I'm being unnecessarily dramatic, for Saturday Nights extended to the young, genuine, good times. If they also inflated their tender, vulnerable, palpitating hearts with warm anticipation, that was to be expected. They were teen-agers.

In a generally inhibited time and place, Saturday Nights offered the young both permission and protection to kick over a few low barriers, to be naughty, but not bad. Saturday Night required dressing up, smelling good, and filling your coin purse or billfold with the allowances and earning of the week. Older teens might have a date, but the younger and/or less fortunate migrated to Northlands Ice Cream parlor or the Eagle Cafe for cokes and burgers to ponder, among other things, which song *Your Hit Parade* placed at the top of the charts (of tantamount importance). If someone had been entrusted with the family car these same teens might go to the *Play Mor*, where live music and dancing and an occasional fistfight in the parking lot were the norm. My sisters each in turn had to battle mom and dad for permission to go to this dance hall, and when permission was denied I suspect they snuck out there anyway, because that is where the excitement and the boys were.

Saturday Nights were heavily scripted, of course, and one pretty much mimicked all previous ones, but because they were filled with the yearnings of the heart, they always felt new and never lost their power. And the unspoken hope trembling in a young heart was that *this* Saturday Night might be the one when that special someone walked into his or her life.

Saturday Nights were an investment, and my three sisters were players. The headiness of it all could be quite unbalancing. What else could lead a young woman to gather up a tub of snow on a Friday evening, wrestle it down to the basement to thaw, and then to strain it through a cloth, heat it, and finally to wash and rinse her hair in it, when perfectly good tap water was already available?

Indeed, nothing was simple on the seventh day. Saturday Night demanded bluing in Friday's wash water (or was it the rinse water?) to make the white blouses sparkle. Saturday was unforgiving of wrinkles; ironing was a time-consuming but absolutely necessary part of the afternoon.

For girls, dressing up was a balancing act; closets were small and they had to make the best of a few combinations of skirts, blouses, and sweaters; and more than one Saturday Night was completely and irretrievably ruined by a shrunken pullover.

Through all the preparations for The Night young women knew that sooner or later they had to deal with their rayon stockings and their ornery seams. People of the present age have little idea how a seam up the back of a shapely leg could be so sensuous, but it surely was. The challenge, of course, was to make sure the seam ran straight, and this was no small task. The final event before going out the door was stepping into high heels, hitching up the skirts a bit, turning your back to whoever was in the room, and asking, "Are my seams straight?"

In the early forties Saturday Nights took on incredible poignancy because of the war. Month by month young men and women, who should have been enjoying Saturday Nights, were being shipped off to fight the enemy. Month by month their numbers on the street dwindled until over sixteen hundred from the county had disappeared. The older youth and young adults said their periodic goodbyes, and everyone carried a burden of worry. The younger teens had each other for the time being, but the threat posed by the far off fields of battle simply added urgency to their time together. Patriotic parents stoically accepted the madness which began claiming their children, convinced that the war was a necessary thing. As familiar names and faces began to appear in the local paper under the heading, "Killed" or "Missing in Action," mourning, too, became a part of Saturday Night. Before the insanity was over, fifty-six from the county died, mostly on foreign soil.

Chapter Twenty and a Half

Saturday Night Two

We are like slaves in search of shade,
we are laborers longing for our wages.
God has made my days drag on and my nights miserable.
I pray for night to end, but it stretches out while I
toss and turn.
My parched skin is covered with . . . dirt and sores.

Job 7.2–5, CEV

Saturday Night was one thing for the teenage crowd, but quite another matter for the farm families of the county. For the latter, Saturday was shopping day. The timing varied with the seasons and the state of the fieldwork, but the overall routine changed very little. Dad gassed up the Pontiac and loaded the eggs into the trunk. Mom stacked the dirty dishes and threw a dishtowel over them, pulled her shopping list from the pocket of the bank calendar, and herded the small children into the back seat of the car. Then dad started and pointed the car toward Pipestone.

Town meant Pa Jones, Sacks, Red and White, or the Red Owl store to buy groceries. Or Demary's Hardware, Montgomery Ward's Farm Store,

Gambles, or Walkup's Farm Implement to meet the mechanical needs of the farm. For those overalls, sheets or shoes one entered J. C. Penny's or Silverbergs or S and L. Though most of these no longer exist, in those days Pipestone had it all.

Saturday was about shopping, but much more. The precious evenings were for bumping into people to complain about the torrid heat, or to talk farm machinery, or to exchange the latest gossip, and to count on the fingers the months from the new mother's wedding day. But that wasn't fully it either. Saturdays were stroke-hunger therapy. It was the primary antidote for the sterilizing virus visited upon the average farm family by history, the Church, society, and hard circumstances.

The hunger emanated from a world in which sweat, weary bones, dust grinding between the teeth, and grime layering on the neck and behind the ears, begged for a reprieve. A world in which the farmer squinted at the rising sun through open barn doors, then labored under its dust-filtered power through the heart of the day until shadows lengthened at last into dusk, reminding him that the milk cows waited at the gate just as the aproned and equally weary wife waited in the kitchen with table set and ample meals carefully prepared, but often too long from the stove, meals wearily eaten with perfunctory complaints about the lack of rain or drop in corn prices, which at last gave way to falling into a cramped bed close under the heat-trapping ceiling in a one-window upstairs bedroom possessing a pillow with no cool side but lumps to be periodically pounded out in between tortured dreams where finding the money to pay the mortgage took the form of grasping at spider webs, and all this before dawn brought the routine round once again. Saturday? It beckoned like a temptress. It led farmer and farm hand alike to wait their place in line for the washtub of cooling, graying water to bathe away the accumulated dirt and sweat of the week. And, no matter how long, hot, and laborious the week had been, a bath, a clean set of clothes, and an eye towards town rejuvenated both body and soul. Everyone had energy for Saturday.

Yet, it wasn't as uncomplicated as that. In my youth, community had not yet fully come to Pipestone County. Parents of the average farm couple had brought with them from Europe centuries' old ethnic barriers. The early immigrants settled largely in tribal enclaves, the Dutch here, the Swedes up the road, and the Germans across the township. People attended ethnic churches, held ethnic picnics, and harbored inherited ethnic suspicions, and just because you occasionally met the neighboring farmer at the fence line, that did not mean he was your neighbor. A generation before my time the two may not even have shared a common language.

The same strict European background and the independent life of the farmer created men who would admit to no fears or needs, and women who carried no expectations of tender moments or expressed sensitivity from their husbands. This culture permitted little physical contact between the sexes, and none between the men. As late as 1969 when Norma and I moved our family to a small, rural community in Western Minnesota, the two of us became objects of gossip because we walked the streets of the village hand in hand. We had no idea we were violating community standards, and once we found out we went walking more, attempting to offer new options and a little permission for others. To our knowledge, we affected nothing. This was about the time the afore mentioned chiropractor told me that 85% of his business was probably from people who suffered no real problems but simply needed to be touched.

So, Saturday allowed a person to literally rub shoulders with others in the narrow aisles of the Gambles or Ben Franklin stores. It permitted shaking hands with people you had not seen for a time. And small wonder dancing was so popular. It offered one of the few legitimate avenues for acceptable, physical contact. But not for everybody, because religious restrictions got in the way. Just as the Catholic Church still convinced its members that sex was for procreation only, so Baptist and Evangelical and Methodist churches offered confusing double-messages about life and promoted hearty inhibitions against alcohol, card playing, and almost anything else that might lead to someone having a good time. Most especially did they frown on dancing, which led a later, reactive and exaggerated generation to ask, "Why can't people from around here fornicate standing up?" The answer. "Someone might think they were dancing."

It was a time and place where, for reasons of blind propriety, God often moved among us unobserved, and people walked around with pious faces to feign innocence for sins hidden. We worshiped a God who was like "Old Dutch Cleanser." He carried a stick and chased dirt.

We now know that babies who are not touched, die. We know that baby monkeys, deprived of a mother monkey, will cling to a wire mesh and rag substitute, but that these monkeys grow up sterile. Without touch, life ends in one or two generations. Certainly among the good people of my youth, life suffered for want of touch. And yet, many babies were born, so how bad was it? And what do I know?

Of course, I'm generalizing. In our home dad was always affectionate, and he was a man of sweet words. Certainly he was not alone. And my descriptions most certainly are overdrawn, AND, we were, indeed, a society of the physically inhibited. I still bear some of the scars.

So, Saturday, and Saturday Night, contributed to keeping people "alive." Even if it offered but meager physical touch it provided the next best thing, psychological stroking. "Going to town" was essential to good health.

Chapter Twenty-One

....

Body Parts

Few sounds pleasure me more than the laughter of children being naughty. I speak of those moments when "in the other room and out of sight" they band together to risk breaking some rule where nothing suffers but the rule itself. The resulting delight is impossible to mistake.

Growth and learning lean heavily on naughtiness. Unchallenged, rules become heavy-handed, and over time can become the voice of God itself. What we are *taught* becomes rigid within us, sometimes reliably so, but too often to our detriment. In contrast, what we *learn* remains flexible and subject to repeated change. In part, that distinguishes religion from spirituality.

Children are kin to sponges, of course, soaking up their weight in worldly matters every day. At any age, we are defenseless (and therefore innocent) against the spoken word; what we hear registers in our thinking. *Milky Way* candy bar. See, you have no defense. You registered a candy bar in your thinking. But I caught you off guard, so get ready, we'll do it again. *Yellow ball.* You see the problem. We are blank slates. Among the debris that children record are the injunctions, those directives given to them that they are bound to follow. When these are articulated they are better positioned to rebel against them, but many are insidiously invisible, slowly possessing people without their knowledge.

For instance, no one clearly instructed me that the body was shameful, even dirty; yet I grew up with unquestioning certainty that both were true. Boy bodies especially were inglorious. Our Christian religion silently promoted it, though it could not talk about it, and our almost invisible Puritan heritage safeguarded it. My sub-par physical makeup, rife with imperfections through and through, compounded the problem. How did

I ever survive? What little salvation I experienced came through those improperly civilized friends who had escaped the burden of a proper upbringing. They, at least, kept the door to better understanding ajar.

When I was seven or eight I heard the horrifying news that to make babies a man and a woman had to be naked together. I squirmed, my stomach tightened; no way would I ever be seen without clothes in front of a girl. She would witness my shame. In concert with such convictions came the tacit double message, more strongly heard, I suspect, by girls: "Sex is dirty; save it for a loved one." Try as we might we never could quite get it right.

We all, of course, live in worlds of our own making, each one different. One person's sin is another person's virtue. We are born anew every moment, but interpret each gift of moment with the criteria of the past. I grew up in a world where parents never had sex, where ministers never went to the bathroom, and pretty girls never passed gas. It really is important to discover how totally illusional human life is. It's the curse of a highly developed brain.

Even the naughty stories we heard and retold out in the back yard reinforced our convictions. "Pete, Mike, and Mustard" stories were weekly fare. Asexual in the narrow sense, they revolved around bodily functions. In other words, they were "dirty" stories. In hindsight, they may have been helpful in that they permitted us to laugh at the dirt, which sanitized it a bit.

When I was twelve one of my neighborhood friends gained access to a book entitled, *Being Born*. His nurse aunt had left it with his mother, and he snuck it outside without her knowing. A genuinely boring book, it described the body's internal organs, and probably somewhere described the birth process. After much research my friend located a single paragraph describing the sexual act. Told in cold, clinical terms, of course. Two anatomical models in some research lab could have clattered their way through the process at least half as well as we humans. Without bending a joint. In truth, the book was written for sexual manikins, some of whom, incredibly, never saw their lifelong partners naked.

We innocents were guided by the times, by religion, and by our own accumulating ignorance and fear. For me, much of this masqueraded as religious wisdom. Again, no one sat me down to teach me this, but very early I understood that proper actions were the mortar that held my world together. When a fourteen-year-old friend declared one day that he wanted to commit adultery, I felt anxious. I was not sure what the term meant, only that it was properly forbidden, and I could not fathom why anyone would want to break one of God's commandments. If they were not kept sacred, then all else became endangered.

The friend never lost his intent, however, and the next year, in the back seat of a 35 Ford, with one friend driving and another trying not to look over his shoulder from the passenger seat, he accomplished his great sin. With a poor girl who had been a virgin once upon a time. The next day he reported to a gaping band of neighborhood kids, including me, that it hadn't been all that great. Under the circumstances, it's difficult to imagine otherwise. Thankfully, the world did manage to hold itself together in spite of his profligate excursion.

When I joined the Air Force in 1952 I learned that attitudes regarding hormones varied across this country. I also came to appreciate what an inhibited, some would say, "backward," I would say, "wonderful," part of the country I came from. For instance, Gary, my room mate in Russian Language School, hailed from Rochester, New York, and he described an upbringing where sexual activity was part of growing up. His descriptions and expectations of life seemed both insensitive and disrespectful to me. People used people, lied to them if necessary, and had little appreciation for fidelity. That's the way it was. He laughed in disbelief at my reaction when I said people from Minnesota didn't act that way. Being a bit of bumpkin, I honestly believed it.

I've pondered my teen-age years for this chapter. I've realized that I and my best friends talked about girls on occasion, but indulged little in sexual discussions, nor did we evaluate girls in overtly sexual terms. With the possible exception of Chub, we were too ignorant to do otherwise. Chub is suspect because he occasionally plopped down thirty-five-cents for a lurid paperback. Still, outside of his one time suggesting that so-and-so, a so-and-so a year ahead of us in school, had probably had sex with his girl friend, I recall no other discussion. In fact, I dismissed Chub's troubling suggestion; people in Pipestone High School didn't do that.

I checked out my surprising recollection with Woody, one of my two, constant, high school companions. His memory matched mine. Five weeks ago I met with a high school friend whom I had not seen in over forty years. As we talked about tooling around in my dad's 37 Chevy, he commented on the same thing. We did not reduce girls to sexual objects. We did fantasize "making out" however, which meant moving from holding hands to hugging and finally to kissing. The mere thought of that was sufficient to put us on tiptoe and warm our insides. A kiss was its own rich reward and not an invitation for anything more. The rules leading up to that first kiss were fairly well understood. Girls seriously discussed it, boys generally respected it. One could reasonably expect to exchange a kiss at the end of the third date, alas, something none of us experienced.

My stronghold of sturdy inhibitions became a fortress through growing religious beliefs. They were not the same, but they did dovetail nicely. For instance, one did not commit the sin of fornication, nor cause a loved one to do so. To suggest to a girl that she might engage in sexual trespass would have been an insult to her, and not to have been faithful from birth to the one you would someday marry was infidelity, pure and simple (It took me many years to discover that some women considered a proposition as something other than an insult.)

Clearly, my generation was both soundly cursed and richly blessed. In one package. With hindsight we recognize how burdened and backward we were, though most of us have freed ourselves sufficiently from the injunctions to be comfortable with ourselves now. Still, we sometimes regret that so many lines have been erased, and continue to be thankful for the expectations that directed us, even if sometimes poorly. The guidelines were more important than their content, you see. The world cared enough to give them to us.

Indeed, when my generation gets together we laugh at the way we were, and give thanks for the stability of the world then. In the mean time, we have grown enough to freely laugh at the punch lines, if they are not too sordid. And to our credit, they sometimes are. We may have been dull dates, but our honeymoons, if a bit clumsy, were exciting with discovery. We somehow managed to get ourselves naked, and in time, to start families. But not before we had taken long walks together, or experienced the intimacy of holding hands, or sharing dreams and uncertainties, or spending a Sunday afternoon or two going through each other's family picture albums. For the most part we skip-roped our way through the process in fairly uniform fashion: *First comes love, then comes marriage, then comes baby in a baby carriage.*

Most of us have built lives and raised families with the person with whom we started, and together continue to grow into decent, unencumbered people--something I celebrate at every high school, class reunion. Our learning has long ago superseded our instruction, and injunctions have been discarded as the excess baggage that they were. Yet, we have hung on to just enough inhibition to occasionally experience the joy of being naughty, though the world offers a skimpy menu of rules to break. Fortunately, we were given so many that some of us have a few left over.

Chapter Twenty-Two

Junk Man

For years the North End endured a solitary salvage man who could be as cold and vicious as a treble hook. Day by day he unloaded and sorted and piled and loaded iron and steel by hand, and the exertion molded him a rock-hard body. His thinking, too, seemed as rigid and unyielding as the metal he dealt with, and he maintained and nurtured a dark and abiding anger. He was the kind of man who would stumble over his own feet and curse you for it. He bulled his way through a variety of community problems of which he was the common denominator, and these problems he carefully cultivated because from them he hammered out his identity. It was him against the world. He filtered everything through suspicion and a seething irritation that did not hesitate to shake its fist in the face of God or anyone who walked the earth. Everyone who crossed swords with him came away shaken if not physically hurt, and I knew of several people who feared him.

My relationship with him was one of distance—I kept as much of it as possible between the two of us. I stood in awe of him. I once saw him unleash his two-fisted fury on a mountain of a man whom he knocked down and then kicked at least twice. His savagery that day convinced me he was not above picking up a piece of pipe and beating someone to death.

He vented his rage on me once when I was sixteen, shaking his large, iron toughened, fist through an open car window and in my face; and I was afraid, and ashamed of my fear, and angry at myself for being so. When I got home I vowed that never again would he shame me, that I would take any kind of beating to avoid that. And then prayed to God that my resolve would never be tested.

Chapter Twenty-Three

Common Courtesy

Two events a half-century apart. One happened last night. The wind-swept temperature hovered around zero. Norma and I were driving home from Pamida when we noticed she needed gas, so we pulled into Casey's to fill up. Now I married a woman who never needed liberating. Her boundaries are clear, and she buys into none of this world's sexism (I married much better than she did). So, even though she is free to enjoy having car doors opened for her, she pumps her own gas. Still, she and I occasionally play a game. In severe weather she will stand out in the blistering wind pumping gas while I sit in the warm comfort of the car. She makes a big, visual deal of being the disadvantaged half of a lopsided, chauvinistic relationship. If she seems to be gaining an appreciative audience, then I attempt to counter her "move" by clumsily crawling out and "painfully" hobbling to the front to check the license plate or something, all the while leaning on the car or holding my aching back. In truth, we trade off doing the "chores" for the other and find ways to have fun while doing so. One kindness deserves another; you just don't keep track.

Actually, last night I pumped the gas. Norma went inside the store to pay. After hanging up the hose I drove to the front door so she would not have to walk the greater distance back to the pump island. The woman behind the cash register was so taken by all this that she commented to my wife, saying how lucky she was, and that she didn't see "that" very often. We both were surprised by the observation. Has common courtesy really become so exceptional that it deserves comment?

The other event took place in a long, narrow cafe on a Saturday after-noon in Pipestone. It was during the war years, and I was about ten. This particular cafe disappeared long ago and I would have no recollection of it except for this one, barely remembered event. I can't recall the cafe's name but it possessed a counter that ran along one side, with booths filling in the space on the other. Traffic flowed in the aisle between.

I and two adults occupied a booth. As our rural mail carrier passed by on his way out, he met a woman and tipped his hat. One of my companions commented that he, the mail carrier, was the only man left in the county who automatically tipped his hat to the ladies. A few others still did it, but for him it was a regular and well-intentioned courtesy. Both the comment and the man's polite ways made a lasting impression on me.

And time marches on. From common courtesy to courtesy uncommon. Each succeeding generation has shucked overboard the niceties and small decencies of the grandparents. What in our generation can we any longer describe as genteel? Who even knows the nuances of the word? Gentlemen (an outdated term) are too little gentlemanly, and ladies often are not ladylike. Yes, I know how sexist that sounds, but the truth is, I miss people being courteous, I miss people dressing up, I miss having a sense of decorum in gatherings. Modesty and good taste seem rare; people unable to distinguish the difference between revealing themselves and exposing themselves, all too common. I shudder at the boorishness I see in so many places, and . . . and . . . yes, I hear myself and realize I've become an old fogey who craves at least a modicum of elegance in life. I like soft edges, and am having trouble finding them. So in my life style, I try to create them, and in the process am becoming a bit eccentric. And what does this have to do with memoirs of my early years?

Chapter Twenty-Four

Shiny Copper

I was sixteen and tooling around after dark in dad's work car, a respectable, if tired, 37 Chevy. This black car usually was available to me in the evening, and I emptied its gas tank a couple times a week. Old Liz, as we called her, was the drive-in movie vehicle of choice because of its special feature. The back part of the back seat was hinged at the top like a door, and raising it up provided full access to the trunk. Of course the door swung both ways, so to speak, and we could secret two, even three, people in the trunk, go to the Sunset Drive-in, and once past the ticket booth fill the back seat with movie goers before we reached the parking attendant with his flashlight.

The biggest obstacle to making this work was me, because I would feel so guilty, and assumed I looked guilty. I was convinced the ticket booth crew could look right into my cheating heart, and consequently, into the trunk. On occasion they would shine a flashlight into the empty back seat, and I always expected them to pull the unlocked trunk open, but they never did. I didn't like doing this but couldn't deny my fundless friends the expected helping hand. Thankfully, our chicanery was never exposed.

Anyway, I was tooling around after dark with Woody and I forget who else, and as we approached highway 47 Carol Karlson passed by in her dad's 49, blue Mercury with a car load of girls. Intent on following them I swung out onto the highway without pausing at the stop sign. Police officer Ford also was out tooling around and saw what I did. Very quickly, red lights flashing, he pulled me over.

Shining his flashlight into the car, he said, "Ignoring stop signs tonight?" I had no answer, and he then asked for my driver's license, turned the flashlight beam on it, looked at me and said, "You Sam Gist's boy?"

"Yes."

"Uh huh. You think your dad would be proud of you if he saw you driving like this?"

"No." I felt like a little boy under his scrutiny.

"I don't think so either,"

He then studied me for a donkey's year as I became less and less comfortable, which was probably his intention. Then he said, "I'm not going to give you a ticket, but I expect you to drive the way your dad would want. Okay?"

"Okay."

And that was it.

The same officer later stopped me another time for speeding following a basket ball game, and that night he said he was going to take each of us home and put us to bed, his way of saying it was time to get off the streets. But, again, no ticket.

Many talk show hosts derided (still occasionally deride) Hillary Clinton's book, It takes a Village. "Raising a child is the parents' job," they argue (Of course.) "The problem with people today is that they don't take responsibility for their own kids" (Perhaps). Still, looking back it seems to me that mom and dad got an occasional helping hand from the village because it, too, felt responsible. Many of the people around us cared. Even the cops, about whom we so consistently and unfairly complained.

Chapter Twenty-Five

Testimony Time
(What did you expect?
I'm a preacher)

All of us are on a spiritual pilgrimage whether we call it that or not. Each event, every experience, becomes a spiritual root from which we draw our understanding of life, a sense of ourselves, and if we are so inclined, our vision of God. Each life is a story that becomes part of God's story, and only as both are told and heard do we begin to understand either. Sadly, many people die without ever having the chance to tell their story, to come to know that their life is significant to the whole.

We begin with beliefs that are handed to us. Unfortunately, when beliefs become deeply rooted they become oblivious to counter beliefs and examples. They bind us into a small arena of the vast Universe, blinding us to the unending data that come to us. The Church has burdened each of us with certainty, and with "experts" to insure the certainty. Consequently, spiritual and personal growth are an unlearning process, a breaking free from the stranglehold of well-meaning instruction, and moving into necessary uncertainty. Sometimes painful and frightening, growth often leaves us with little to hang on to. Paradoxically, for that very reason the Church remains important to me, even though its set ways stubbornly stand as barriers to growth. It is that steadfastness that has upheld me during a lifetime of asking questions.

One time on a spiritual growth retreat, the leader had each of us lay on the floor with a pillow under our heads. We were to imagine the pillow to be the lap of a very wise, old woman who read us a children's story (which the leader did). The process was remarkably therapeutic, allowing each of us a few precious moments to relax into our inner child (When I've told this story to people I have given myself license to actually rest my head in the lap of this very wise old woman, but, alas, it didn't happen that way).

When I am troubled, sick, or in pain, I become emotionally much younger, and God alone knows how many times I have crawled into the lap of Mother Church to be nurtured and reassured. There I rest among familiar answers, even some I have rejected, and by them I am sustained. As contrary as I can be, the Church remains my home. Like the love I had for my father, which led to arguing with him, so with the Church. I always have found cause to challenge it. Yet, the Church constitutes my spiritual family. I could never desert Her.

This is a bit curious because I reject the basic tenet of the Faith. For decades I have been unable to accept St. Paul's version of the "Good News," because I have been unable to accept the bad news he based it on. The bad news: that God does not accept me just the way I am. I'm so lovable, how could God not? God's love is unconditional. The "Good News" is not centered in a cruel execution needed to satisfy God's blood lust–how absurd–but in a resurrection, whatever the early Church meant by that–and it varied with the writers. So not everything the Church offers me is nurturing, but still it is my Church, for many reasons.

The Church taught me to pray, "*Our* Father" (or Mother). The idea of a private, or a strictly Christian God, will not fly.

The Church entrances me with its, "In the beginning, God . . . ." Who can imagine a beginning? Life is couched in enticing mystery.

It offers the symbol of humble service, of Jesus kneeling down to wash his friends feet.

It breaks the spiritual life down to "going about doing good," a concept I can embrace.

It speaks of a God who is "with" the sparrow, and that is a God I can celebrate.

It says with a voice I identify as divine, "Follow me."

It insists that justice and righteousness are God's plan, and that they will work.

It humbly declares that we are to learn from the children and the non-human nations of this world.

It speaks, not of nature, but of Creation; every place is holy ground and each new sunrise cause for rejoicing. Under the layers of rigid doctrine and self-serving theology, at its best the Church recognizes the holiness, the wholeness of existence that honors each and every fidgeting molecule.

Additionally, the Faith teaches me through a *Domini* what the highly touted and misunderstood, *dominion*, means. People entertain the notion that Nature is God's gift to us to use as we wish. As though Creation is not about glorifying the Creator. All nature sings the praises of God, and too many people too easily silence the worshiping voices. We kill too easily. But our *domini* taught that power is to be used *under,* never *over*. In a real sense we are the servant species.

The Church surrounds me with a family that knows how to give, in a world where too many people measure success by how much they can make or take.

And it stands by its declaration that God is love.

I grew up in Zion Evangelical Church. When the church building was constructed, some genius incorporated into the wallpaper immediately over the recessed sanctuary, a burning torch. This "light" stood behind three serpentine scrolls bearing three words: "God . . . is . . . Love." They were attractively done up in gold and silver, a combination a child could not ignore. As an often bored little boy who faithfully was brought to worship each Sunday, I pondered those scrolls. The letters were in elaborate Gothic or Old English, and it took me years to identify, first the letters, then the words. That accomplished, I understood each word separately, but not as a statement. What exactly did they mean? I never was exactly sure but I read them thousands of times. They became a part of me. The words come from St. John, of course, a writer who in other places was downright unloving. But here, he got it right.

During the fellowship time following dad's funeral I sat across the table from John Meyer, a lifelong friend of our family and most especially of dad with whom he played softball. John grew up in Zion too. As we sat there I mentioned those mysterious words on the scrolls and how they had become a part of me through repeated readings. John perked up and nodded. He knew what I was talking about. He, too, had sat on those hard pews Sunday after Sunday, repeatedly reading and puzzling over those words. Every church edifice should have those words attractively emblazoned in full view of the children.

Who can clearly identify all the ingredients making up the complex whole of a spiritual life? All things contribute. This book is little more than a recounting of some of the incidentals that molded me spiritually. In my adult life I have known profound "spiritual experiences," each one of which changed the direction of my life, AND, it is the day by day experiences that slowly define our spirits.

As youngsters we are so busy with the task of growing up that we too little think in spiritual terms. On the other hand, I can point to the first, consciously planted step of my own journey. I took the little used *Victor Mature* route. The date was August 9, 1951. I and Don Johnson walked to the *Orpheum* to see Mature and Hedi Lamarr in *Samson and Delilah*. Poor

Victor often was panned as an actor, but he did a sufficiently good job as Samson to convince a sixteen-year-old that God was a God to take a stand for. Someday. On that date I offered my first intentional prayer, telling God that I wanted to live a meaningful life no matter what the cost. This was kept between the two of us, of course; it wasn't something "the guys" would understand.

About this same time I found on my radio people who actually seemed to get excited about God. One was Oral Roberts, the other, Ace Allen from Miracle Valley, Arizona. Allen was beamed all the way up to Minnesota in the late hours of the night through the might of a super-powered Mexican radio station. He preached with that raspy, breathy voice so popular among southern evangelists, a voice that somehow translated into fervency, and fervency was sister to unquestioning faith. Anyone with such blazing confidence had to be genuine.

Besides, he was a healing minister; he had the power of God at his command. And he used his preaching skills to beat on the sins of the human family. Most especially he ranted against Demon Alcohol. No one in my family drank. We didn't exactly call it a sin (though our church did), but already by that age I considered it a weakness. If someone needed alcohol to feel good or have a good time, they did not have much going for them (Each morning I patted a little face makeup on the emerging blue on my nose.) I applauded Allen's passion, and so fortified myself against strong drink that it never became a problem. I still do not know the taste of a beer, and I dislike the smell of it on someone's breath. I did get around to having a drink of wine at my fortieth birthday, and have since sampled a few mixed drinks. Norma and I predictably go through two or three bottles of wine a year, though neither of us enjoys the taste of it, nor do we experience any good feelings from it. We reserve it for guests.

You can imagine my disappointment when I read in a 1952 *San Antonio* newspaper that A. A. (Ace) Allen had died in an automobile accident, drunk behind the wheel.[3] I had not yet learned that preachers who consistently rail "agin" some "sin," are typically the ones fighting that particular demon themselves. I don't mean this as an indictment, but rather as an observation of human nature. Allen's preaching was a prime example of projection, and projection becomes perception. He was not dealing with himself, but seeing the problem elsewhere. We see this often in religion. The news media over the years has provided us with the tragic examples of such people that are too easily and quickly labeled hypocritical. There is more to it than that.

---

3. Allen was a controversial person, and however it happened, the report was false. He did die years later (1970), however from liver failure brought on by acute alcoholism.

Still, the ways of God continue to surprise me. Words in the wallpaper. A tragic figure mightily preaching over the airwaves. Victor Mature as a spiritual stimulus. Who would guess? Yet, in spite of many years of seeking my truth, and often being gently waylaid by the Mystery, I realize that the single greatest, spiritual, influence in my life was my father. A man who could barely read. A man who to my knowledge never read a page of Scripture. A man with whom I never once had a religious discussion.

What I learned came from his consistent pattern of interpreting the world around him as good. For instance, as a teenager I one day stopped by his mechanic's shop and the two of us went out for coffee. In the coffee shop three men in an adjoining booth boisterously talked (so all could hear) about a local "loose" woman. They described her sexual antics with the precision of a participant, and quickly left her underfoot, thoroughly disgraced. Once we were back at the shop I asked dad if he knew the woman. He said yes, and then added, "She's a nice person." When I commented about the boorish behavior of the men in the other booth he cautioned, "They're not so bad." That was all. Dad consistently viewed people as persons of worth, in spite of themselves.

It was that message that always presented itself to me in the Gospels. The call of the Christian was to treat others as God's beloved children, without separating judgment. Through that simple act God would work, in spite of ourselves.

It took another five years after having coffee with dad before the power of that was fully demonstrated to me. I was in the Air Force and stationed at *Misawa Airbase* in Japan. Among our numbers was a Christian zealot who regularly launched himself into town where he would target a nightclub. He was so on fire for Christ that he repeatedly made an ash of himself. This young man would commandeer a place on a stage, and from that pulpit beat people with the printed word, adding his sure commentary that the Heavenly Father was fixing to send them all to hell. I never was able to merge the concept of father, earthly or heavenly, with the notion of designed suffering, and considered his approach to be detrimental to the Faith. I never met this man, but his reputation was unavoidable, and I marveled at his *chutzpah*.

For the uninitiated, the people in the towns and villages around US military bases quickly learn that servicemen spend awesome amounts of money on liquor, entertainment, and women. The village of *O'Misawa* was typical. A town of a few thousand people, it contained 104 bars and boasted 400 licensed prostitutes. The "lowest order" of prostitute was the street hooker. As you walked through town they met you, grabbed you by the arm, and tugged in the direction of their room. Each knew a few, key American phrases, and seemingly a lot of American curse words.

The first time I went to town a young woman approached me, and (ha!) I was flattered. Never had a female, girl or woman, had designs on me, and even the first, commercial come-on hooked something in me. AND, I knew who I was at that point. I said to her, "What's a pretty girl like you doing in a profession like this." Honest. I was there. I heard me with my own ears.

She promptly cursed me in English and said, "Don't try to flatter me, G.I." We both moved on.

My next time down town she again presented the hard smile, offered herself, and I politely declined and tried to make conversation. She quickly moved on.

This pattern repeated itself two or three times more. One evening she sought me out and when I greeted her, she promptly said, "You don't go with street girls." It was both a question and a statement. I said no, I didn't, and she said, "That's good," and turned away.

The next time I went into town she ran to meet me. I almost did not recognize her. Her face was soft and glowing and her smile genuine. She said, "I have present for you. Open your hands." She then gave me some peanuts. At that moment something akin to friendship surfaced, and never before had my Christian Faith felt more validated. I remain forever aware of the difference between the professional smile of a prostitute and the soft smile of a potential friend, and am left wondering how one might settle for the former over the latter.

The young woman's name was, *Yukiko*, which someone told me meant, "Snow Flake." I don't know if that is true or not. I've never wanted to question it, for it adds a delicate touch to the memory. Two or three days later I again went to town, and Yukiko was nowhere to be found. In fact, the world of prostitution had been totally transformed. Over night the male bosses had moved all four hundred of "their girls" to another base town and replaced them with four hundred different ones.

I never saw Yukiko again, but she pulled me a step further in my journey. The spiritual pilgrimage consists largely of opening doors within, living with discomfort, standing breathlessly on tip toe, and awaiting the next surprise from God. We can do little ourselves but to respond to the active Mystery, which emerges from wall paper and movie screens, confused preachers and rigid doctrine, someone's wise grandma and people in the next booth, from mom and dad, and zealous, young preachers, and yes, *Oriental* prostitutes. God is God over all of it.

Chapter Twenty-Six

It was the worst of times, . . .

I sometimes stand appalled at our human capacity for cruelty. To others and to ourselves. Why do we so easily deal pain to the people we love?

As the trailer in our family I was in competition only with the youngest of my three sisters–Shirley. We are a few months shy of being five years apart. By the time I was ten she was in those awesomely fragile, adolescent years: the time of self-doubt and self-criticism when we compare ourselves to all the perfect people in the world and come up woefully short. Every blemish or imagined blemish becomes life diminishing. How can we go on living when we are so homely, so unattractive, so stupid? We typically define ourselves by our imagined limitations, and lucky are those who escape that trap.

I became my sister's tormentor. With that radar we all possess I quickly focused on her vulnerabilities and with the accuracy of smart bombs, delivered heavy and destructive payloads into her thinly shielded ego. Why? Was I luxuriating in newfound power? Perhaps in part, but just as much it fell into that category of clumsy intimacy that I shared with my dad when I argued with him. It was the heavily disguised face of love masquerading in petty meanness. I truly loved my sister, and yet my "play" was her torment. I repeatedly grabbed her by the wings and stuck pins into her. She sometimes reciprocated, though I have no memory of her ever getting mean.

Our combative moments might revolve around something as innocent as a piece of cake. If I thought she had her eye on a particular piece I would touch it. Horrors. I was infectious, I was unclean, and she would never eat anything I touched. Nor would I eat it if she touched it. Each of us was devotedly germ conscious.

Cake was fun, other things not so much. For example, all I had to do was look at her and nonchalantly touch my finger to the area beneath my nose. That was sufficient to send her into considerable emotional pain, because I had convinced her that when she smiled this area became disfigured. She came to "see" just such a blemish, such is the power of imagination. She began throwing her hand over her mouth when she smiled to hide the flaw. And I considered myself a nice kid. Of course, as is true of most siblings, I would rise to her defense should anyone else say something about her. I never let her know, of course.

Do the gods chuckle or weep when our cruelty revolves back around to ourselves? If I helped create a tormented teenager in my sister, in time I also did a magnificent job on myself. Let me explain.

At a Christmas, family gathering several years ago the conversation settled around two of our children who have been diagnosed with OCD (Obsessive-compulsive disorder). The OCD is not debilitating for either one–each is successfully employed and socially active–and it has become something of a family joke. When someone is acting a bit irrational a common response might be, "Is that you or the OCD talking?" On this particular occasion, however, I said, "I wonder where it came from?" All my children burst out laughing and pointed their fingers at me. This was the first time I ever considered that I was a "victim and carrier," but it almost immediately answered questions I have had about myself and my mother. I always felt that mom worried herself to an early death at the age of 56 (actually, heart disease ran in her family). She had a great capacity to agonize over things that troubled no one else, and I suspect she created many sleepless nights.

OCD may also explain much of my own behavior that I have been critical of over the years, behavior that says I don't cope very well with life. For instance, virtually any challenge makes my mind go blank. I could never be on a television quiz show because I would make a fool of myself; even though I might know some of the answers, they would disappear temporarily behind a blank screen. When someone expects something of me I go into a small panic, convinced I cannot produce, and so will fail them. In college, in spite of being an "A" student, I would anxiously fidget in class nurturing the fear that I would be called upon to respond. It was crippling. Over the years I have worked enormously hard to know myself and to grow in many ways, and yet my children had no compunction about pointing their fingers at me, mostly because of my germ consciousness. I find that amusing. Basically, I'm fine, as long as you don't ask me what time it is.

So with new eyes I can share the following story, though I am embarrassed about it. What became the biggest rock in my stream, affecting virtually everything that flowed by in my teen years, and even beyond, was unknowingly placed there by Mr. Truax, our sophomore biology teacher. He introduced us to "the ugliest wrestler in the world"–"The Swedish Angel." His name was Phil Olafsson, and he had a pituitary gland disorder called *acromegaly*, which caused the bones in his hands, feet, and head to grow larger and heavier in distorted ways. Like mine were doing. I had big, heavy hands and wore a size 7 5/8 cap (I still do). I shortly concluded that I had this dreadful disorder. Any doubts I may have had were dashed when Barb Beggeman wrote in my school annual that spring, "Best of luck to the guy who knew more about birds, bugs, and everything than anyone else. Too bad you didn't know about yourself." My God, other people also knew I had the disease. They must be discussing my changing appearance behind my back. That's why the girls sit in the back of the room and giggle. One day while playing pool with Louie Conrad he marveled at how big my knuckles were. That was his discrete attempt to tell me I had the disease, no doubt about it. Dear God, I would be forever ugly, growing more so, day by day. In time young girls would run screaming at the sight of me and young mothers would shield their children's eyes so they would not be frightened. I would become a laughing stock should I ever entertain the idea that I had the right to expect some girl to accept a date with me. I can't overexaggerate (is that a word?) the living hell I created for myself. Was it OCD, or just hypersensitive adolescence? Go along with me. Let's blame it on the disorder.

Add to this grotesque, evolving monstrosity that was me the curse of cold sores, which I describe elsewhere in this book, and you have all the makings for a very unhappy youth. And that's the most curious thing of all. If my teenage years were the worst of times, they also were . . .

"... the best of times"

Chapter Twenty-Seven

In spite of the ways I found to torment myself I cannot remember ever being unhappy. The time simply was too full of yes and yippee to succumb to the insane onslaught I made on myself.

Three things were substantially true in my life, a fourth beginning to emerge. First, I enjoyed unconditional love at home. I need not say more about that. Second, the community I lived in offered both permission and protection to become and be a teenager, a marvelous gift of circumstances. Third, I had good friends, and the freedom to explore my world with them. The fourth was a tantalizing sense of the mystery of life hovering just beyond my fingertips, a beckoning towards what was not yet, but also what could be. (I now know this to be the final, and often frustrated, fourth stage of brain growth).

About this time I had what I considered a most important dream. In the dream I sat at a small fire with three other individuals. One, a religious figure; another, an artistic one; and the third, vague and unknown. The fire slowly was going out, the darkness correspondingly creeping in upon us. We were sitting there dying, knew we were dying. When the fire went out, that would be our end. Suddenly, I jumped to my feet and said, "This is silly. I'm not going to sit here and die when I can get up and live." My action allowed the other figures also to get up and leave. That vague figure followed and slowly has taken on definition as my spiritual self. I was becoming aware of it in the shadows already in high school. I'm still working to bring it fully into the light.

I speak of my parents and the town elsewhere. What about my friends? Among them on the North End was Herb. Herb came from a family of gorgeous sisters and handsome brothers, attractive people, all. Herb had the eye of an eagle. He could throw marbles into the air and shoot them with his 22. He also could send poor, bounding, cottontails rolling in the snow, catching them in mid hop, and at considerable distances. Again, with the 22 rifle. At that stage of my life I loved hunting and wanted to be as good a shot as my dad, or as Herb. They both were great, I, just average.

Then there was Larry. Larry was a couple years younger than I. I never entered his house and knew little about his family, but he spent many hours in our home and cars. I taught that slender, blonde-haired kid how to play chess, and on our seventh game he beat me. Thereafter I could not match him. I remained an average chess player, he became a good one.

The best belcher in the neighborhood was Terry. He was five years younger than I, but still a good friend. I never learned the art of burping, much less belching.

There was Don. Late one afternoon when I was sixteen I took my customary short cut through his family's yard on returning from town. Donnie met me in the driveway. Distraught as I never before had seen him, he told me he accidentally had shot John, our friend and neighbor. In admiring some handguns kept in his house, he had emptied them of bullets, and then he and John played "fast draw." After he reloaded his dad's 38 police revolver to return it to its place, John cried, "Draw!" one last time. Before he realized it he had raised the pistol and fired, catching John in the left shoulder. A moment later John's mother called to say supper was on the table, and she very quickly called the ambulance after hearing that John was down. He was rushed to the hospital, and in time fully recovered. I waited with Donnie for the difficult task of telling his parents about it when they returned. That was as dramatic as it got in the neighborhood.

Donnie and I grew up together. He was a year older and always much bigger than I, as much as sixty pounds at one point. The first time I "slept over" with him he warned me that often, while still asleep, he would go into a rage and beat his pillow like a mad man. That sleepless night was about as scary as it got in the neighborhood.

Other good friends included John and Roger, brothers and my most frequent playmates; Denny and Norman, and a bit further out, Harold and Richard, all of whom contributed richly to my existence. In later years one of the last two was imprisoned in California for rape, and the other allegedly sent to an army stockade in Germany for murder. But when we were young, they were just kids, just friends, struggling to grow up under difficult conditions.

If Herb had the remarkable hand-eye coordination that made him a great marksman, Donnie had the eye for angles. I loved the game of carom billiards and longed to become good at it. I never did. Donnie, on the other hand, became as good as anyone who played the game at Harry's *Pool Hall*. My game plateaued at "average," his ascended to the heights.

"Harry's" was a second home to us after we were old enough to enter its doors. Actually, it was the "Royal Pool Hall," an attachment to the Royal Hotel. Harry Houston rented and ran it.

The first time I saw Harry he was on his back at the quarry, a cigar in his mouth and an open magazine in his hands. On the water. He was made of cork. When he jumped into the water he would barely submerge, and then would bob up, head and shoulders above the water. He delighted in floating out to the middle of the quarry, putting a straw hat over his face and graying, balding head, and taking a nap. Or so he claimed to be doing.

In time Harry became a genuine friend, and he would leave me in charge of his pool hall on a lazy summer evening while he drove to Sioux Falls to see his beloved *Canaries* play baseball. One morning he was nothing short of jubilant as he showed everyone who came into the hall the foul ball he had caught the night before. He displayed it behind the bar for the rest of the summer.

His "hall" was truly that in the physical sense of the word. Long and narrow, it sported two billiard tables, a huge snooker table, and four pool tables, and Harry hovered over the action at each like an anxious hen. Although he sold no liquor, a substantial bar graced the front end of the hall. From behind it he would dispense pop and candy, and always there were wieners slowly turning in his hot dog machine. In all the time I spent there I never had one of his dogs. As far as I could see he had no place to wash his hands, and when he pulled a bun apart and cradled it in his hand to receive the wiener, all I could see were germs. It amazed me that it bothered no one else.

My folks were not too excited about me spending time in a pool hall, after all, it began with "P," but Harry's was a friendly place, frequented by farmers in the off seasons, and by decent town folk the year round. I never saw so much as a scuffle in the place, and consequently, never saw a blue uniform there either.

I don't know how large a police force my hometown now has, but I know it has grown substantially. In contrast, when I was a child Louie Breed and Ed Moe shared a single police car working alternate twelve-hour shifts seven days a week. In the late thirties a third officer was hired so eight hour shifts were possible, but still seven days a week. By the time I was driving I think there were three officers plus the chief, and some part-time help. Still, that was thin coverage for a community of five thousand. AND, it was sufficient.

Too often on television we see documentaries of scam artists ripping off senior citizens. They are easy pickings, not because they are old or stupid, but because they are unguarded. They grew up in times and places that engendered trust, where people respected others and their property, where hand shakes finalized bargains, and at least in the towns, the streets were policed by well-known neighbors. What a sad commentary on our times that many see decency developed in those years and places as a weakness to be ruthlessly exploited.

The reality is that once upon a time a kid in bibbed overalls could lean his bike against a tree most anywhere in town, and come back hours later and find it there. People left keys in unlocked cars, and when they went out for the evening left the house unlocked. In Pipestone, I and my friends often went to Harmon Park after midnight and turned on the court lights and played tennis until 1:30 or 2:00 a.m. The police would drive by, but never stopped to suggest we should be going home, because they knew we were no threat to the community. We all enjoyed a security and freedom based, not on doing whatever we wanted, but rather on respecting the rules and regulations that governed and steered our shared life. It's a simple concept, but one many people either don't understand or refuse to abide by. Freedom never is doing what one wishes, but rather living fully, with respect for individuals and community.

When I entered tenth grade I developed my first, good friendship with someone from the other side of the tracks: Harlan Fletcher Clark, better known as "Chub." We shared a passion for checkers. On a winter's evening we would settle at the dining room table in our home and play until two and three in the morning. Thirty, forty, even fifty games. He would beat me three times out of five, his devilish satisfaction escalating with each new tactic he developed, especially in the game of "giveaway." Chub was a good checker player. Me, only average.

In the summer of 1950 I secured a three-week job working for the Rock Island Rail Road, laying down new, heavier tracks. They paid the handsome wage of $1.12 1/2 an hour, almost four times my hourly, thirty-cent salary at the Hiawatha Market. Daily I, and a new kid in town, Roger Paul Wood, were given the dirty task of setting spikes for the husky workers who drove them in with air hammers. We would get the spikes started by pounding them into the tie enough to make them stand up, the drivers would finish the job pneumatically. They delighted in pushing us hard and hammering the spikes right behind us, setting up clouds of dust for Roger and I to eat. The two of us would sabotage them by setting the spikes so loosely with our mauls that they would fall over when the pneumatic hammer was dropped on them. Out of that hot, dry ordeal we bonded, and I developed a rich and lasting friendship with "Woody."

Once we were laid off I went through my paycheck quickly, breaking the last twenty-dollar bill at the bowling alley on the third Saturday following. To my utter amazement Woody made his last into the winter. He was a good money manager. Me? Not even average.

At this time Chub and his brother Harold worked for a shingling crew out of Edgerton, and they came home only on weekends. When I told Chub I had met a neat new friend he was his typical, skeptical, "show me," self. But very quickly after getting together the three of us became inseparable.

It was at this time I discovered a valuable truth. If you draw a line on a sheet of paper, one way to make it longer without touching it, is to draw a shorter line next to it. I realized that if I surrounded myself with shorter lines I could improve on my mediocrity, and wonder of wonders, I discovered that I was a better bowler than either Chub or Woody. I determined at that moment to keep them as friends and to go bowling often.

Roger's dad, B.Z., worked for Northern Natural Gas, which transferred him to the work in Pipestone. Farmington's loss was our gain. I considered Woody the best kept secret of our class. Too few people came to know his marvelous wit or charming ways. His warm, frequent smile under a mop of black hair was obvious, his great sense of humor had to be experienced. Roger looked and acted like his gentle-mannered mom.

That fall Woody bought a "Sixty Ford." The "60" referred to horsepower, not year. The car could not pull the hat off your head, but it did get us to Flandreau, South Dakota on occasion, and even around "the square" in Pipestone a few times. As I think back, we didn't use his car nearly so much as the Gist vehicles, most certainly because Woody preferred to save the gas. He was maddeningly practical.

Chub, on the other hand, was just maddening. He enjoyed being contrary and still states his opinions as though they are facts. He lived with his fraternal twin and mother in a small house on Third Avenue East. The twins moved in two, totally different social circles, agreed on nothing, and fought about everything.

The Clarks did not have a car, so their home became our meeting place, Woody and I each driving to that point. Chub's mom, Bertha, took great interest in each of us and always involved herself in our give-and-take. Yet, she had the smarts to stay in her role as an adult, never intruding into our activities. Indeed, all of our parents liked each of us, and were comforted, I'm sure, knowing that we would not get ourselves into serious trouble. None of us drank, and because we all talked fairly openly, they came to know the kind of things we were about.

We never were very creative with our time, but we always filled it. A typical evening would include a stop at Harry's, then repeated "circlings of the square," checking out the girls and stopping here or there for a soft cone or a coke. Infrequently we each bought a pipe or cigar and puffed an evening away on those, but none of us took up cigarette smoking.

To fill the later evening hours we might go to the Sunset Drive In movie theater for a double feature, which would put us back on the streets well after midnight. On many occasions we then stopped at the park to play tennis. Because each of us was a "short line," our games were always competitive.

Once in a while we would finish up a night by going swimming at the quarries, but most often, by holding "Ladies Aid." We would park, most usually in the Gist driveway, and just talk. Nothing serious. Nothing life-altering. Just talking. It was healing for teenage doubts, ambrosia for growing spirits, and probably as enlightening as it was irritating for Mr. and Mrs. Stolte, whose open bedroom window was scarcely fifteen feet from where we chattered away the night.

One night Chub fell asleep in the back seat, and Woody and I snuck off in his car and went to Lange's for a cone. We delighted in practical jokes of any kind, and this was just another. We hoped he would wake up and find us gone. He did. And later, when he heard footsteps on the gravel driveway he jumped out of the car and in his most menacing voice, said, "All right, you bastards!" Poor Mr. and Mrs. Stolte were quite startled.

Chapter Twenty-Eight

Skip Day and Beyond

Many a time I got up at four o'clock to go fishing; never so early for a school event. The early hour itself lent novelty to the occasion, the freshness of the morning contributed a lightness. It promised to be a good day. A good Senior Skip Day.

Senior Skip Days were simple affairs in the fifties. They were excursions of relative innocence and decorum, a fun time to put a cap on our scholarly achievements. Skip Day was a rite of passage. We seniors were growing up. So strong was the evidence that we were maturing that the typically staid chaperones—they seemed to have been chosen for their habitually stable, if not grave, demeanor—chose this day to let their hair down and to relate to us less as students and a little more as fledgling adults. The world was "achanging."

Most the of seventy-two members of the "Class of Fifty-two" boarded two Greyhound buses for a five-thirty a.m. start. Roughly twenty-two hours later we would return, exhausted and one step closer to being alumni. This was heady stuff, and yet I remember only segments of the trip. I remember, for instance, how we ended the day at Excelsior Park on Lake Minnetonka, with its rollercoaster thrills, spun sugar and hot-dogs; even high-speed boat rides. I remember Gerald Hunter's pack of cigarettes leaving his shirt pocket as we accelerated down the steepest roller-coaster drop, precisely following our trajectory so that they hung suspended in front of his face, allowing him to simply reach out and recover them. And of course, I remember the highlight of the evening when one of the girl students disappeared with one of the bus drivers for an extended period. Rumor, even innuendo, were quickly birthed over that.

I recall only one thing out of the heart of the day. Not the stop at the Capitol, nor eating at the University Union, nor a visit to the Ford Motor plant in St. Paul. What I remember is that I and someone else, I don't remember who, worked our way, floor by floor, to the attic of some building, and there found boxes and boxes of the "State Boards," the final exam we would take the following week to prove our worthiness to graduate. We were so afraid of being found there that we beat a hasty retreat, with nary a thought of allowing ourselves a sample. We were good kids.

The fuzzy memories of the day contrast sharply with the crisply clear, imprint made at our first early morning stop. Around nine a.m. we pulled into the parking lot of what was indelicately, though officially, listed in our itinerary as "the feeble-minded institution at Faribault." This stop was first added to Skip Day in 52. Whether the class of "53" experienced it, I have no idea. Even though Skip Day allowed us a time away from books and exams, the excursion was in part justified by making it an educational experience, and visiting the feeble-minded was part of our introduction to the greater world beyond home. Indeed it was.

In our short life times most of us had known, most certainly seen, at least one of those people the world labeled "retarded," but it was quite another matter to enter the uncertainties of their world. We had been raised in a society struggling to grow beyond that dreadful mentality that led parents to hide their disabled children in attics and storerooms. Not uncommonly, people were ashamed of their own, and their shame led to unowned cruelty, as well as insensitive language. The State, for all its good intentions, had not yet developed the caring, understanding programs that unleashes the potential and personalities of so many disabled today.

Our visit at the Faribault institution concluded with one, little lady performing for us, not unlike a circus act. She played an accordion, danced, and sang, "I dream of that night with you, lady when first we met." Woody and I, with outrageous callousness, unconscionably mimicked her act for a couple weeks following the trip. Clearly, we had not yet grown up. Still, this was something the woman enjoyed doing and we were told to applaud her efforts because she was so proud of her accomplishments.

This visit began with staff members instructing us about what we would see. Some of the people, we were told, were educable, others, only trainable. At the bottom of the ladder (their words) rested those who were neither; people the State simply warehoused (not their word). We moved through the institutional wings in the order established by the introduction, that is, the last group we saw were those most severely disabled. We filed through a large, gymnasium-like room full of bobbing and rocking, mumbling and screaming, and consistently, almost uniformly it seemed to me, physically deformed people. The room faintly smelled of urine. And right in the midst of it all sat the most beautiful girl I had ever seen. Dark hair, fair complexion, delicately balanced features, about sixteen years of age, she just sat there, seemingly oblivious to the mindless turmoil.

The incongruity of it overwhelmed me, blinding me to the reality that each person in that room had been cheated. I focused only on her. There had to be some mistake. Somebody do something. Let me do something. God, do something. This isn't fair.

A seventeen-year-old was not yet ready to deal with the injustice represented and experienced by every resident in that room, much less that of this single individual, so much like myself, so unlike myself, so lovely. She seemed the victim of some diabolical joke that needed to be negated. And in that appraisal lurked also the awareness that I could do nothing about it. I was willing to mount my white steed and go forth to slay the dragon that kept the beautiful damsel bound, but could not. The world could not. And God did not.

I didn't analyze my reaction in psychological terms, me wanting to play the rescuer. Nor did I reason in theological terms. I just raged at the great injustice involved, not yet having enough life under my belt to bear what I could not understand. Without realizing it, of course, I was confronting the greatest obstacle to a belief in God, i.e., the obvious presence of Evil. How, in a world created by a good and loving God, can such injustice exist? I still struggle with it, as most seriously religious people do. In time we each find an answer that, though it may not be sweepingly satisfying, still allows us to believe, at least in sustaining spurts. My reincarnationist friends tell me she probably chose her existence, either to learn something, or to teach something, or even to work out some negative karma. At the time, that would have been nonsense.

The date was May 23, 1952. I had not yet buried my first, inadequate god. I only knew that suddenly the world had presented another face.

If the school board had wanted Skip Day to be both fun and educational, they had, in part, succeeded.

Chapter Twenty-Nine

Patting Hankies

By the time I came along grandmother Brown—the only grandmother I ever knew, my dad's mother died before I was born—was already old. She wore plain, cotton, housedresses and brown, cotton stockings that seemed always to fall in folds around her ankles. Like Whistler's mother, I picture her in her rocking chair. Yet she had to move about to provide the home-canned peaches and cookies she always placed onto that marvelously worn, round, oak table that sat in the space that doubled as her dining and living room. I remember the goodies, I don't remember her preparing them. Even in old age she was curiously free of wrinkles and I vividly remember her hair. It was reddish-brown and reluctant to grey. She wore it in a bun. Once I saw the bun undone (that's fun to say), and was surprised to see that her hair fell to her waist, which in her case was not all that far. Grandma was short.

Grandma had considerable built-in distance. Perhaps because of her age, or the age in which she grew up. To my knowledge I never sat on her lap. Nor do I have any memories of her playing with me. For sure I was no novelty, with two dozen cousins preceding me in time. Still, she always remembered my birthday, and each Christmas sent me a card containing either a comb or a handkerchief. Knowing that she and grandpa had so little money made these small gifts special. I looked forward to getting them and felt compassionate and protective towards the two of them because of them.

Did grandma dream of better times? I can only assume that she did, but I also suspect that any dreams she held were modest. That was true even of her visions of eternity.

I say that because of one of those religious discussions that occasionally took place around the table. The topic must have been the *Sermon on the Mount*, for grandma mentioned the future promised to the meek, that they would inherit the earth. Then she said, "I wouldn't mind that. It would be nice to have my little house here on earth with maybe a few chickens in the back yard." I remember my mother smiling and exchanging knowing glances with my Aunt Marie, and me feeling irritated because of it. The childlike innocence of gramma's fantasy remains one of my cherished remembrances.

The last memory I have of her is the best. I was seventeen and ready to leave for the service. My mother had a dentist appointment in Walnut Grove and we stopped by my grandparent's home so I could say goodbye to them. I think it was the only time I ever visited on a day other than Sunday. For sure it was my only time in that house when grandpa was absent.

When we walked in—we always just walked in—grandma was sitting in her rocker. A basket of wash sat on the floor next to her out of which she periodically ferreted an item. My mother said, "What'cha doin?" and grandma said, "I'm patting dad's handkerchiefs. He likes it when they're patted." Had I not been there I wouldn't have known what she meant, but she simply took the hankies, smoothed them out on her lap, then folded and smoothed them, folded and smoothed them again, very much like I had been taught to do on an ironing board. Her end product lacked the crisp folds made by an iron, and all of those little wrinkles than an iron chases out remained. It really was not a very presentable job, yet she did it for him because he liked them that way. Long before this I had learned that love is not what you feel, or what you say, but what you do. Love is taking the garbage out so your loved one doesn't have to. Yeah! Love is doing loving things. Grandma loved grandpa.

Chapter Twenty-Nine and a Half

Grace

Grace is of God and the human heart.

Grace most always comes unexpectedly.

The grandmother I never quite knew harbored a secret, one we discovered only after her death. In a newly discovered photograph her father appeared to be Native American. The general White population of her day offered little grace to "Indians," and she for reasons of fear or shame kept the reality of her father secret unto death.

At the time this became known, I was a volunteer chaplain in the emergency room at Hennepin County General Hospital in Minneapolis. One of the chaplains there was an *Ojibwe*. One night over coffee I said to him, "I'm a bit ashamed to share this, but I've just recently discovered that my greatgrandfather was Native American, and it was kept from us because my grandmother was ashamed of it. But I thought maybe you could give me some idea how to begin tracing his family history."

In Jesus-like fashion he did not respond to my question, but rather picked up on my discomfort. He reached over, patted me on the forearm, and said, "Think nothing of it. My grandmother never told us that my grandfather was Sioux."

Chapter Thirty

A New Beginning

Every, single, earthly relationship ends. No exceptions. Being human is totally fatal. That's why the world produces poets, and philosophers, and country music songwriters, to explore and deplore the fleeting nature of life. In another context Frost wrote, "Something there is that doesn't like a wall." Human separation feels like the ultimate wall. We, indeed, do not like it.

"Love" is a word kin to "God" in that we really don't know what either means, and our best attempts to define them are shrouded in failure. We can experience both, but cannot define them. How curious that the Bible offers, "God is Love." What really does that mean? We typically reduce both concepts to nouns, which stops them dead in their tracks. However, both God and love are best understood as verbs; how else can we really experience either? Consequently, this suggests that we might also think of ourselves as verbs, not an easy task. The truth is, philosophers, poets, and theologians, all of us, struggle with the questions arising from these words.

Like children in the dark with flashlights, we shine the word "love" everywhere, and focus it almost nowhere. We love pretty dresses and houses, movies and picnic spots, along with parents and God and life. I once heard a woman say, "I love this parking space," because it saved her from walking an extra hundred feet to a mall.

Many confuse love with need and make impassioned statements of undying commitment, such as, "I can't live without him." And too often we have that "love driven" individual who cries, "If I can't have her, no one can." *Bang!* Such people bring their incomplete selves into a relationship and attempt to live through another, and, of course, it doesn't work. Healthy relationships require reasonably whole people, because, as we clerics are prone to say, "Love is not addition, one plus one, but rather multiplication, one times one. If you take two incomplete people and throw them together, you have the makings for an even lesser relationship. After all, 1/2 times 1/2 equals 1/4." We preachers like saying gimmicky things like that, hoping always that someone might mistake it for profundity.

Defining love is not unlike describing the fragrance of a rose. Words utterly fail us, but shove a rose under our noses and we immediately know that essence. So, too, we may be unable to define love, but believe that when we experience it we surely know it. However, our dismal track record in such matters demonstrates how silly the notion is. Too many "loves" wither more quickly than roses. We mistake the good feelings we get when we are with another as love. But alas, it isn't, and everyone who "falls" in love falls out of love. Standing in love comes with time and work.

Am I going somewhere with this? Actually, yes. Although I did not recognize it at the time, and although I've already said we do not know how to use the word, I still must say that in high school I loved my close friends. If I had identified it then I certainly would never have said it. Not with words, at least. Our understanding of the "L" word certainly was unrefined and filled with notions better left to infatuation, but we would quickly have agreed that boys did no love other boys. Even now it's possible that none of the others would use that word to describe our relationship. For me, it works, and it's fun to ponder the reaction I would have gotten had I said, "Hey, guys, I love you" (Notice how the, "Hey, guys," conditions the word, and how the plural form also makes it less risky).

Chub would have snuffled and looked at me sideways, never bringing it up again. Woody would have accepted the words, but then quickly defuse them by saying something witty, but in a way that would not totally dismiss them. And Donnie may well have said after a pause, "Yeah, you know, me too."

However they are labeled, the close, warm, and fun relationships I enjoyed with my friends quickly led to painful separation following graduation. We barely had slipped out of our commencement robes when Denny Hjermstad announced that he and Harold Wolford had enlisted in the Navy. Both Denny and Harold were good friends and their announcement took us by surprise. It also stirred up within the now mature and educated minds of Donnie, Woody, Chub and me, a hunger for adventure. And the ingredients all were there. The Korean Conflict was in full tilt, we were patriotic, healthy, young Americans, and we had nothing planned for the weekend, so, we, too, would enlist.

Actually, Chub was not a part of our newly birthed enthusiasm; he was off shingling roofs somewhere. We decided it would be a grand joke to have him come home some weekend and find all of us gone, so initially we told him nothing of our plans. Now Chub, like me, had been tailored through the *Civil Air Patrol* to wear Air Force blue, but when he discovered it was my idea to abandon him he was so upset that he joined ranks with Don and Woody and opted for the Navy.

It all happened within a few weeks. Donnie was eighteen and free to choose, but we three younger ones had first to badger our parents into consenting to our enlistments. Then followed trips to Sioux Falls and Worthington to visit enlistment offices, and finally, each in our turn, signed those papers that would dictate our whereabouts for the next four years. Of the six of us who were close friends, only I chose the Air Force. All I could do thereafter to defend my decision was to make barbed remarks about the cute, little suits the others would soon be wearing.

Denny and Harold left in the middle of June. Donnie, Chub, Woody and I hung around until July. We spent our remaining time together doing what we always had done, including an after-midnight, wild wrestling match on the red sand pile at the quarries. The Navy against the Air Force. We threw each other around, tumbling here and there, and in the end the Navy was victorious. In the process I twisted my neck and something in my ear popped. When we later went swimming the water caused great pain in the ear, and I have had problems with it periodically ever since, a lasting reminder of our tussle. As it turned out, this nighttime scuffle was the last, close time we shared.

The three of them were scheduled to leave a week before me, and on the Saturday night before their departure they went to Hatfield with two other classmates who also had enlisted in the Navy, and got stinking drunk (their assessment). It was something I would never do, and it seemed out of character for them. I thought it was rather stupid of them. If it was a symbolic act, the significance of it escaped me. I've never quite understood the process of doing dumb, sometimes childish, things to prove that you are grown up. Even at a young age I was bent that way.

More significantly, even though I would not have gone, I was not invited. This was the Navy's final civilian fling, and Air Force-to-be personnel were not welcome. I was not welcome. With that I realized that the world would be forever different. And I wondered if any of the others cared.

Then, just like that, they were gone. For good. I do not recall that we said any formal goodbyes. I do remember cruising the square without them. I played a few, final games of billiards and snooker with Harry. I talked to mom and dad a little more than usual, tidied up my room, played with Spotty, visited my grandparents, stopped and said goodbye to Chub's mom, and sat through a Bogart move by myself, *Deadline-USA*. It was a week of activity largely void of satisfaction. Indeed, it was the loneliest week of my life. Separation had too quickly come. Only the anticipation of enlistment kept me from exaggerating this new reality.

On July 20, the Sunday before my departure the family gathered at the house. Mom outdid herself preparing all my favorite foods. After dinner everyone lined up in the front yard for a Gist family picture. The gathering then slowly petered out on the well-wishes of my brother and sisters as each returned to their lives.

In spite of my boredom, July 23, my departure date, arrived on time. The night before mom helped me pack, and before breakfast dad had loaded the suitcase into the Chevy. I said my final goodbye to faithful Spotty, and with an uneasy feeling in my stomach, slid behind the wheel of the car.

The trip to Worthington was mostly without talk, each of us lost in our own thoughts. We arrived at the depot with time to spare, and there met other families soberly awaiting the train with their young men. One clean-cut fellow came over to where we sat, and in a most childlike way shoved his arm under our noses and said, "See my new watch." He had received it as a twenty-second birthday present. Because of his friendliness and apparent decency, and because he was more than a kid, mom took some comfort knowing that I would be with him. Once we were officially inducted into the service in Minneapolis the next day, I never saw him again. Perhaps he failed the physical.

Right on schedule the train groaned and rocked its way into the station, and suddenly it was time for goodbyes. I knew mom would want a kiss, something I was not especially looking forward to, but I did manage to give her a quick peck on the lips; then the handshake with dad. Man to man, of course. His son was going off to war.

In truth, I was like a Baptist church without a school bus; things were not yet as they hopefully would be. I still identified myself as a kid, with only limitations to invest. I was marching off to save the world sporting an underdeveloped ego and the unrealistic expectation that I could enlist God in the service of my inadequacies. If I had boundaries I was not sure where they mostly lay. I knew nothing of the greater world, suspected I had much to learn, and slowly was coming to believe I had made a grievous error in enlisting, something the Air Force kindly affirmed for me the very first day of boot camp.

Each of we enlistees threw our luggage into the overhead rack and quickly claimed a dusty seat next to a window. Parents, brothers, and sisters lined the depot platform, eager for a last look at their loved ones. Mom and dad stood next to the depot wall, arms uncharacteristically around each other's waist, waiting for me to appear in a window. Barely had I tugged one open and stuck my head out when the train chugged into motion. I was thankful for that; the goodbye was stretching out too long.

Eastern mystics maintain that beginnings and endings are but poles of the same reality, which means this uncertain event, too, had its yes and yippees. We in the West say every ending is a new beginning, and who can argue with that. New celebrations of life awaited me. In just minutes I truly would be on my own and getting acquainted with other young men I never before had met. The world was opening up. None of that was in my head that morning, of course; I was just doing what my questionable decisions had led me into. In a very short time the events of that July day would recede into the blur of an undocumented past.

All, that is, but one. I carry one ineradicable memory of that morning with me, for the last thing I saw as the train moved out of the station was my dad, standing there, unashamedly, with tears streaming down his cheeks.

July 20, 1952

CPSIA information can be obtained at www.ICGtesting.com
Printed in the USA
BVOW040107060313

314802BV00001B/6/P